MW00892035

This book belongs to

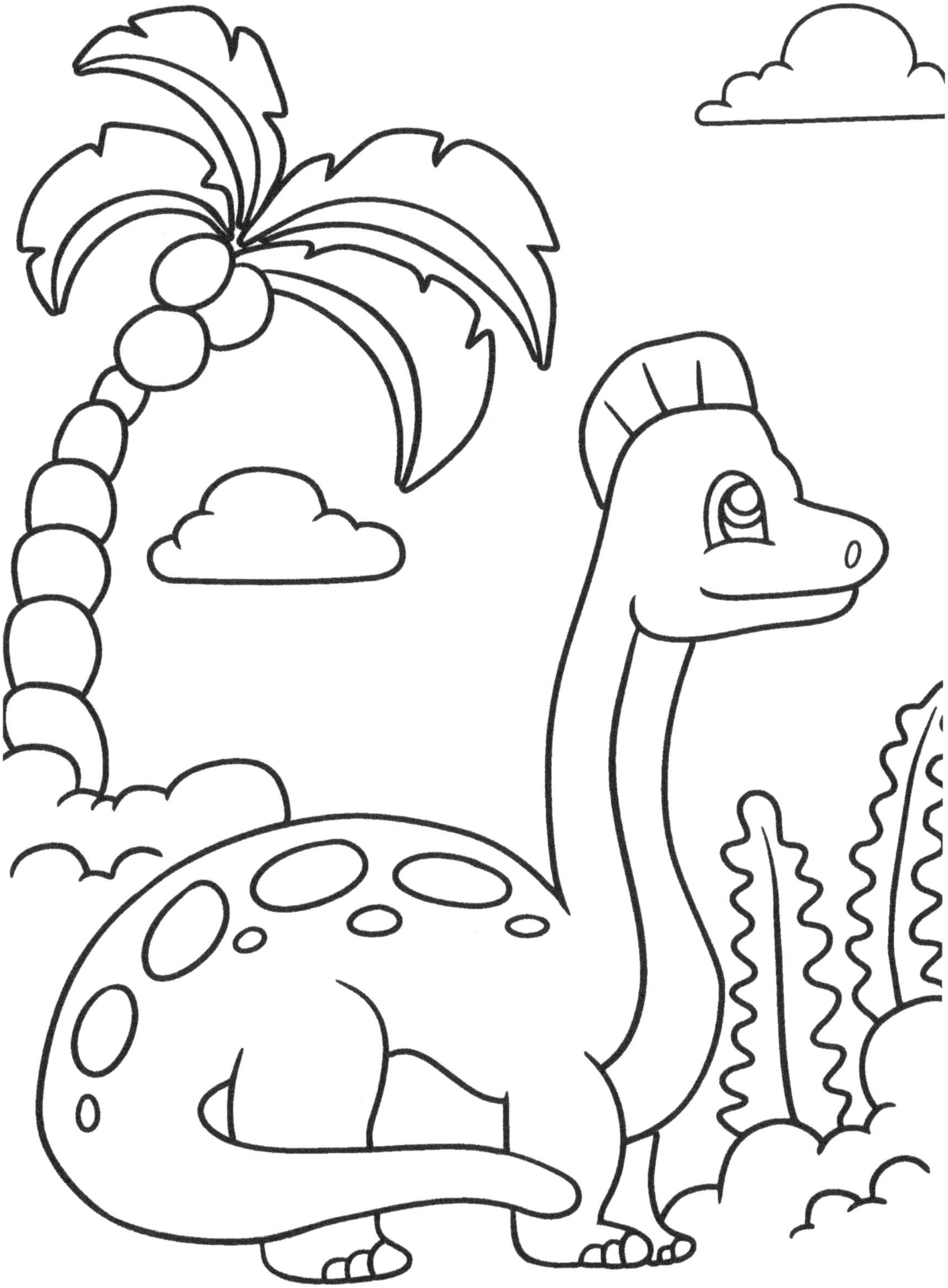

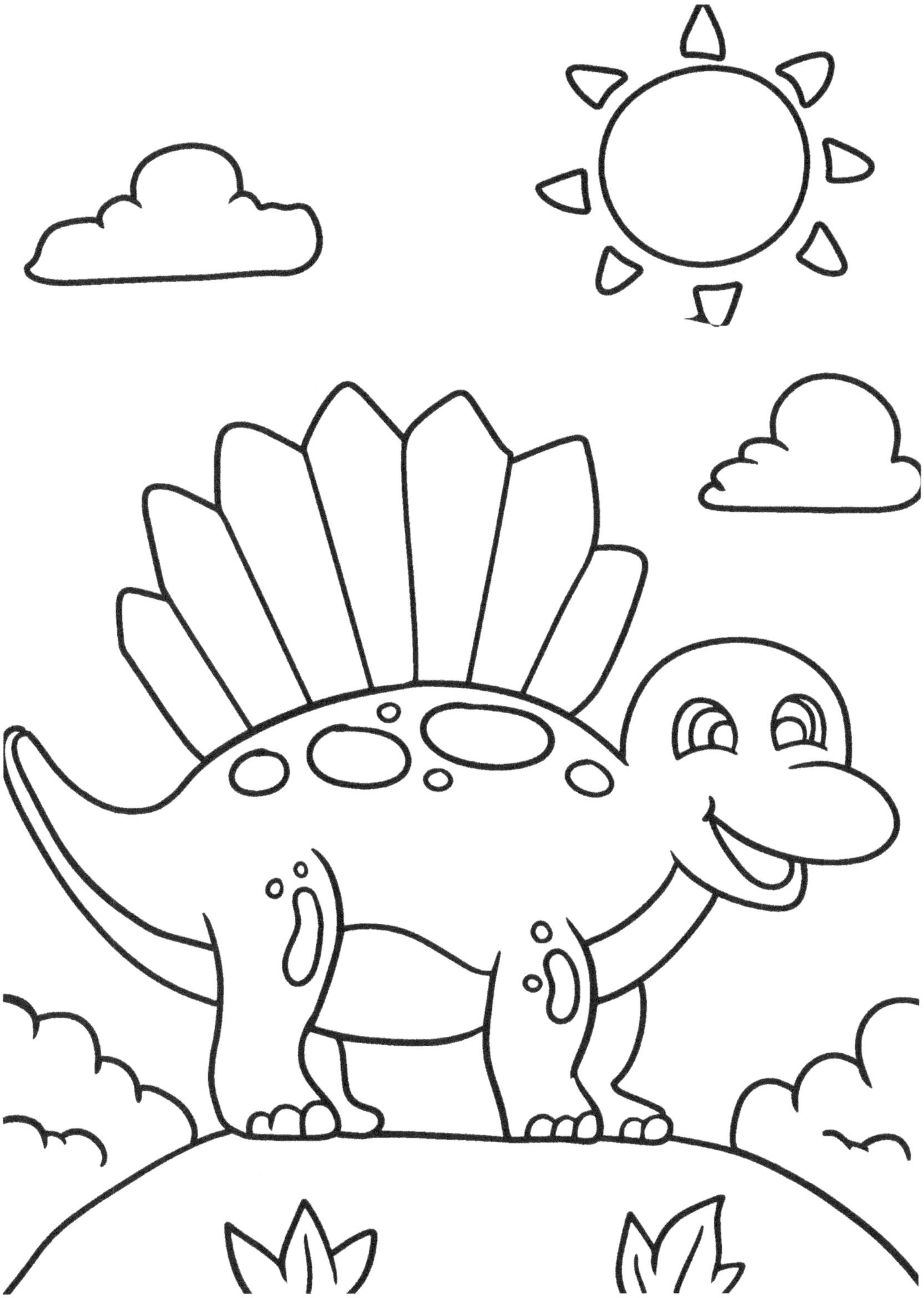

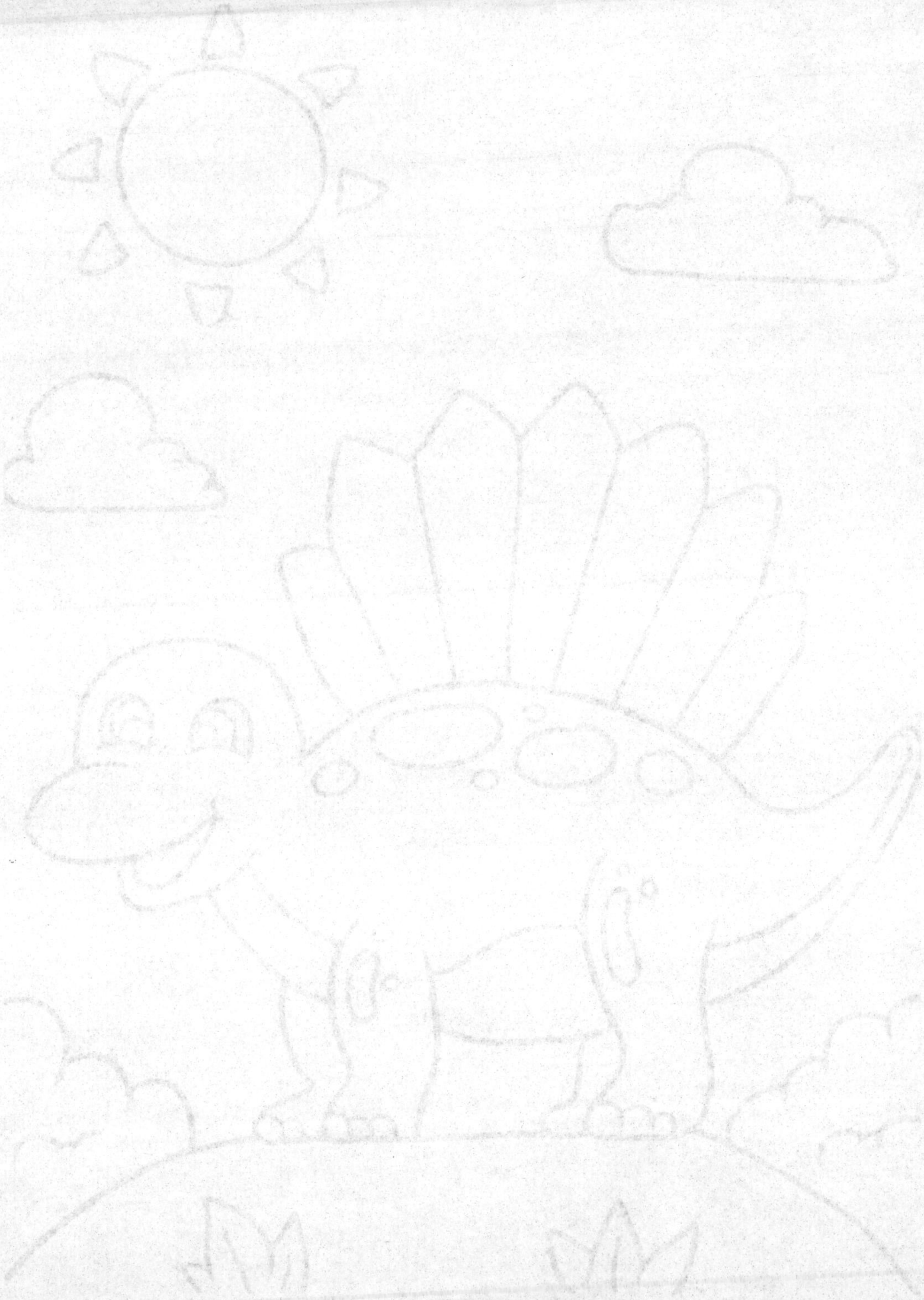

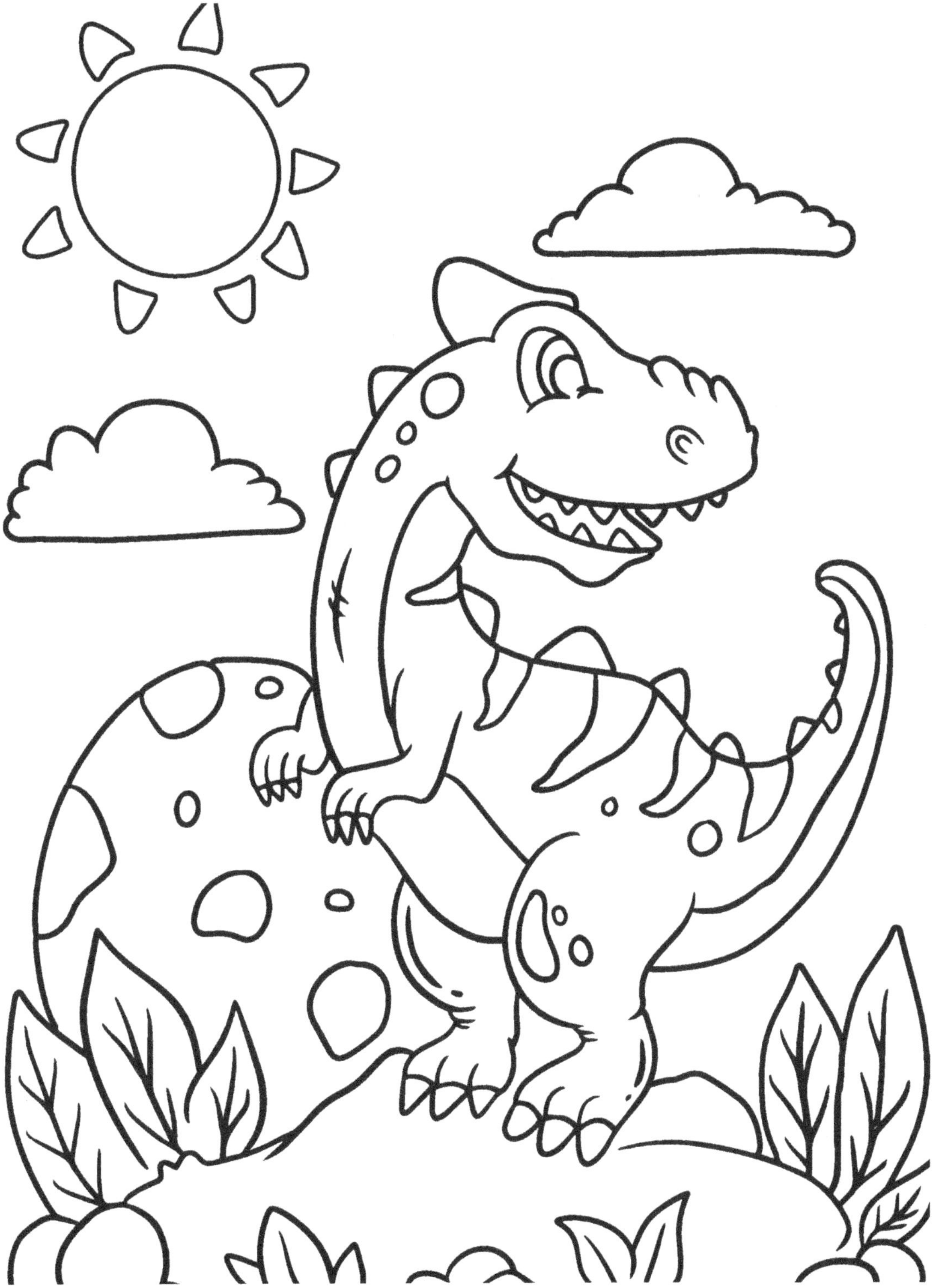

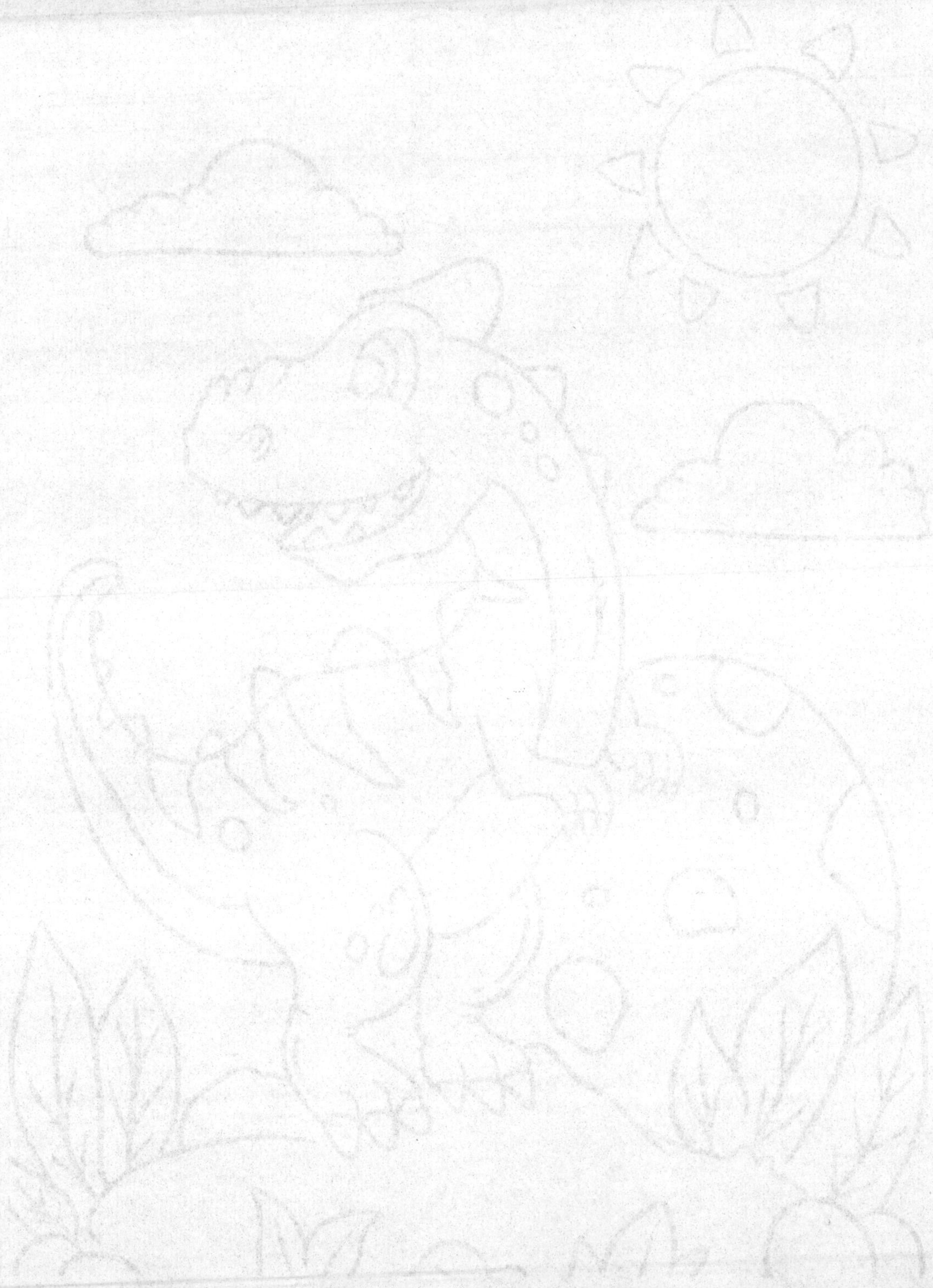

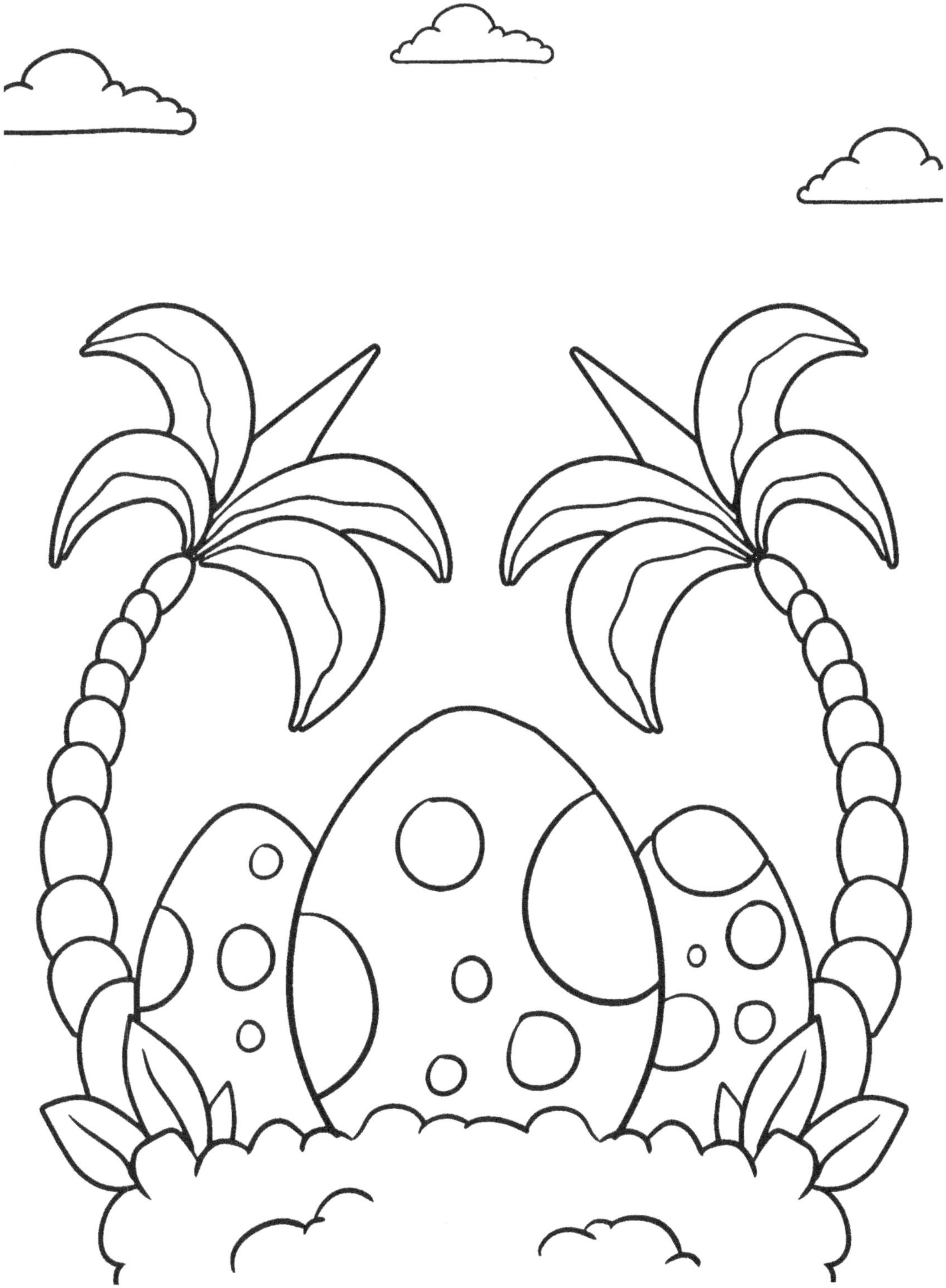

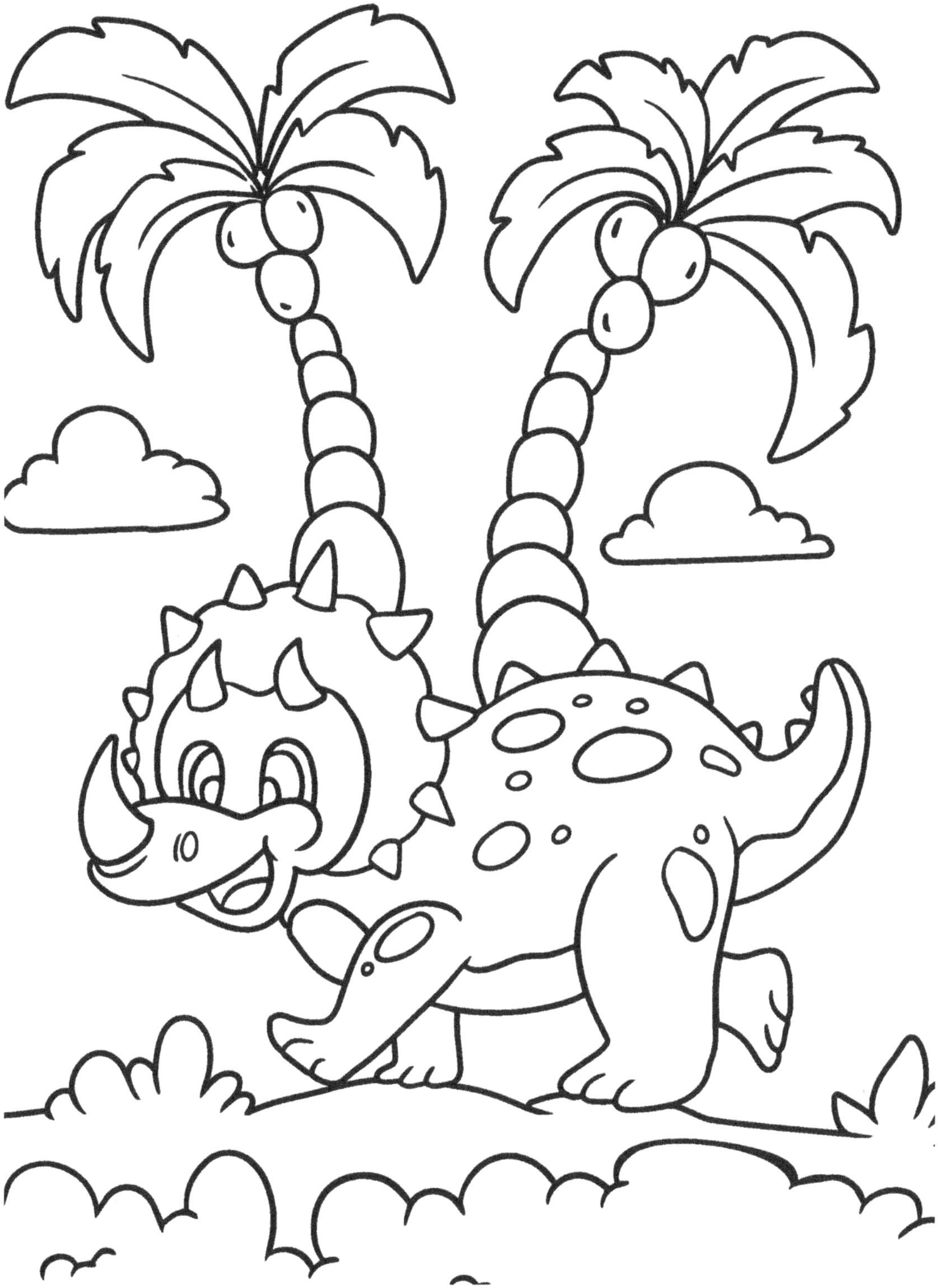

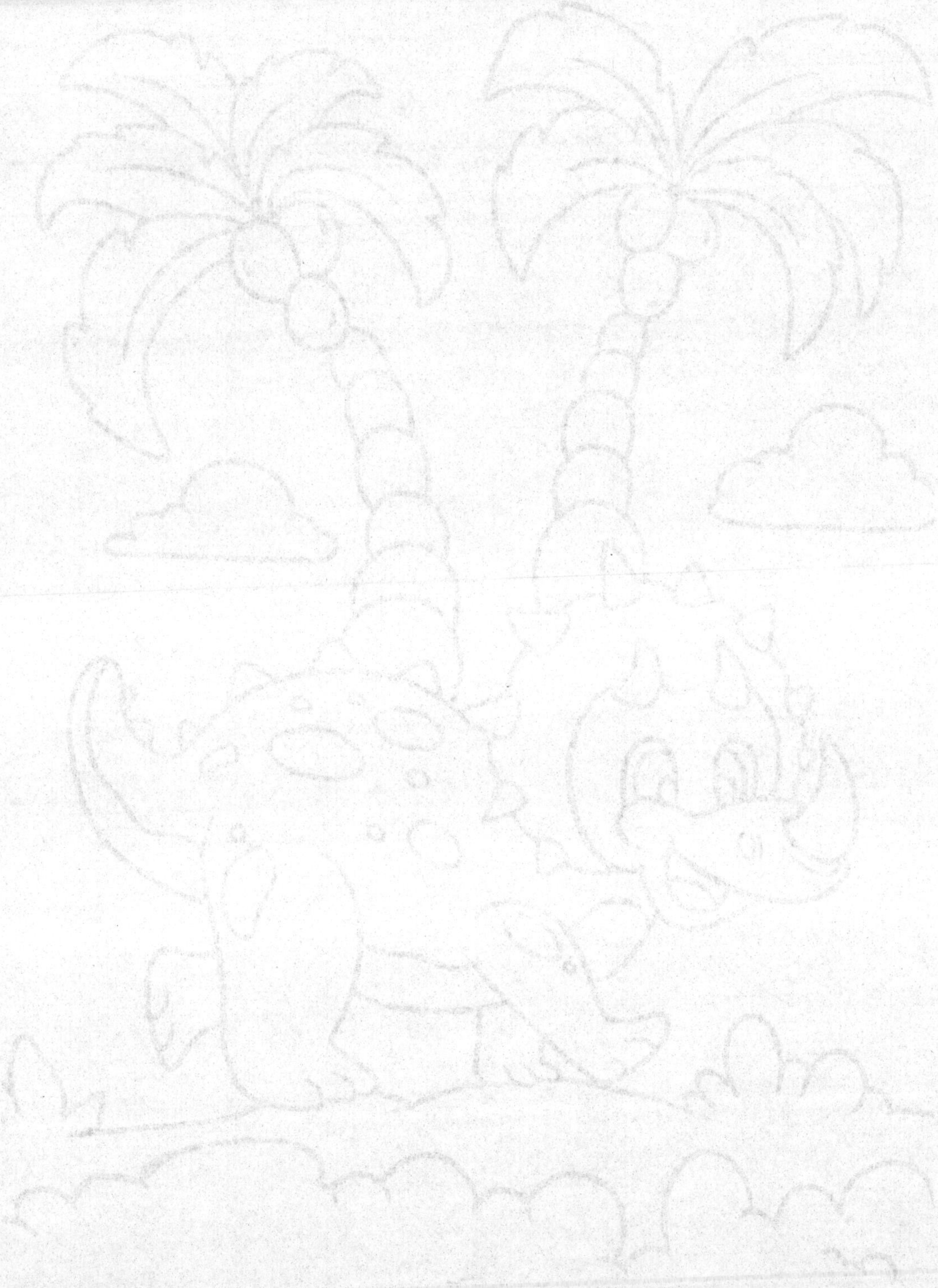

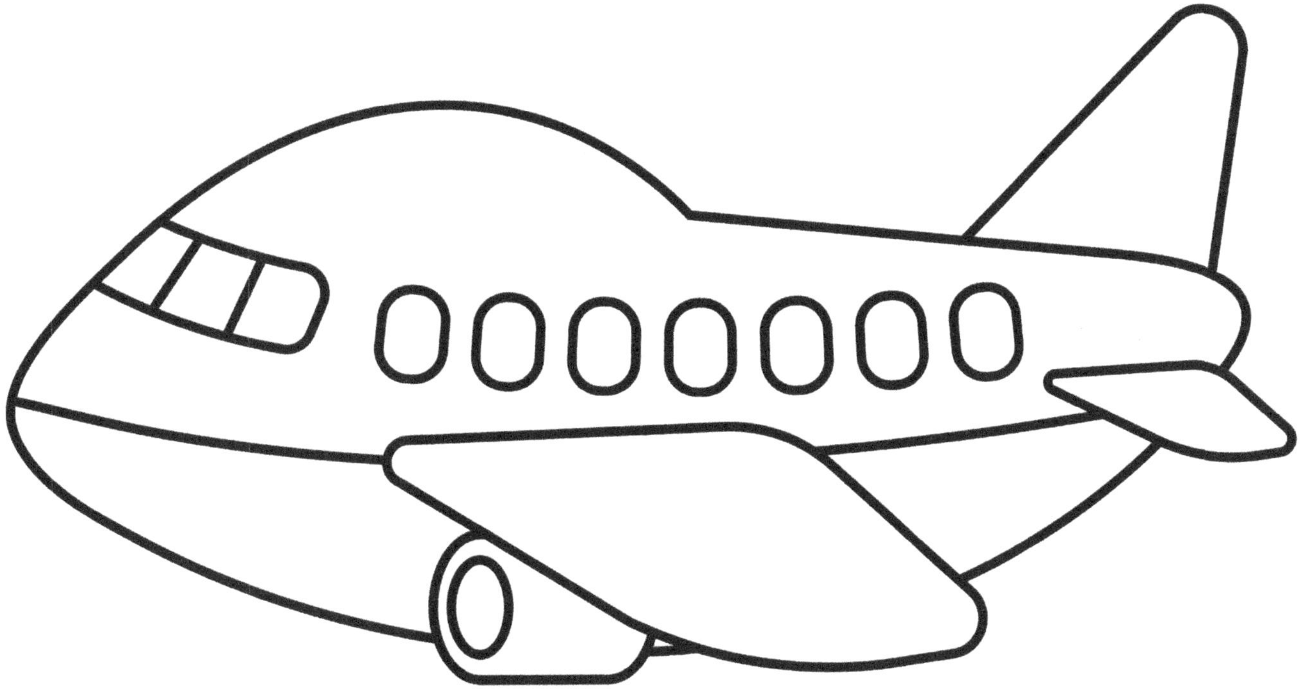

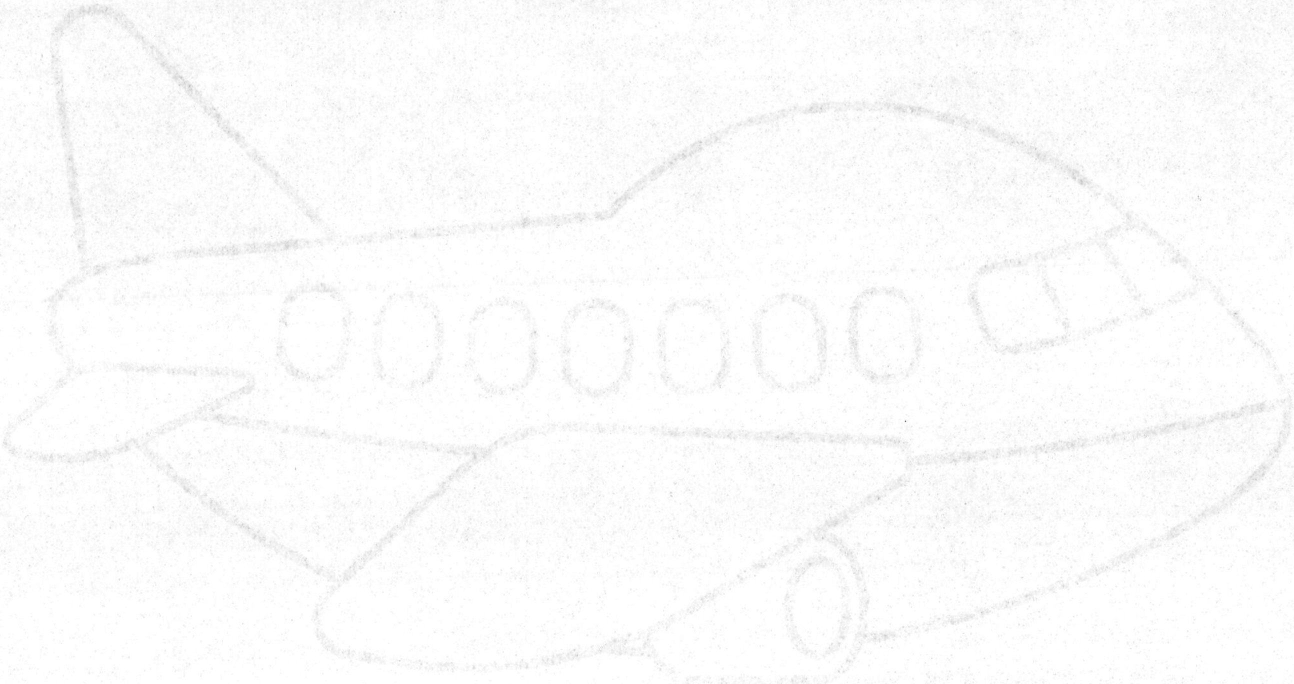

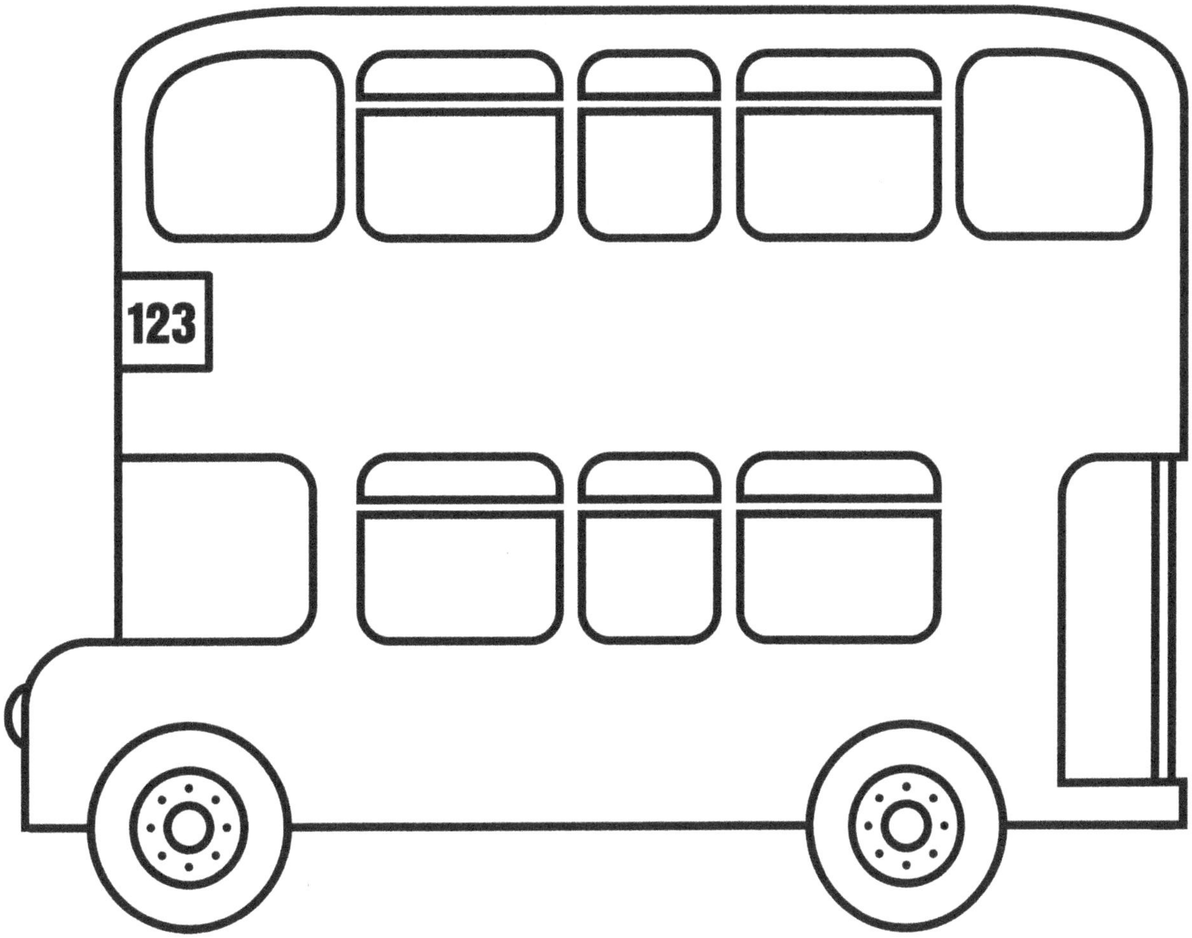
123

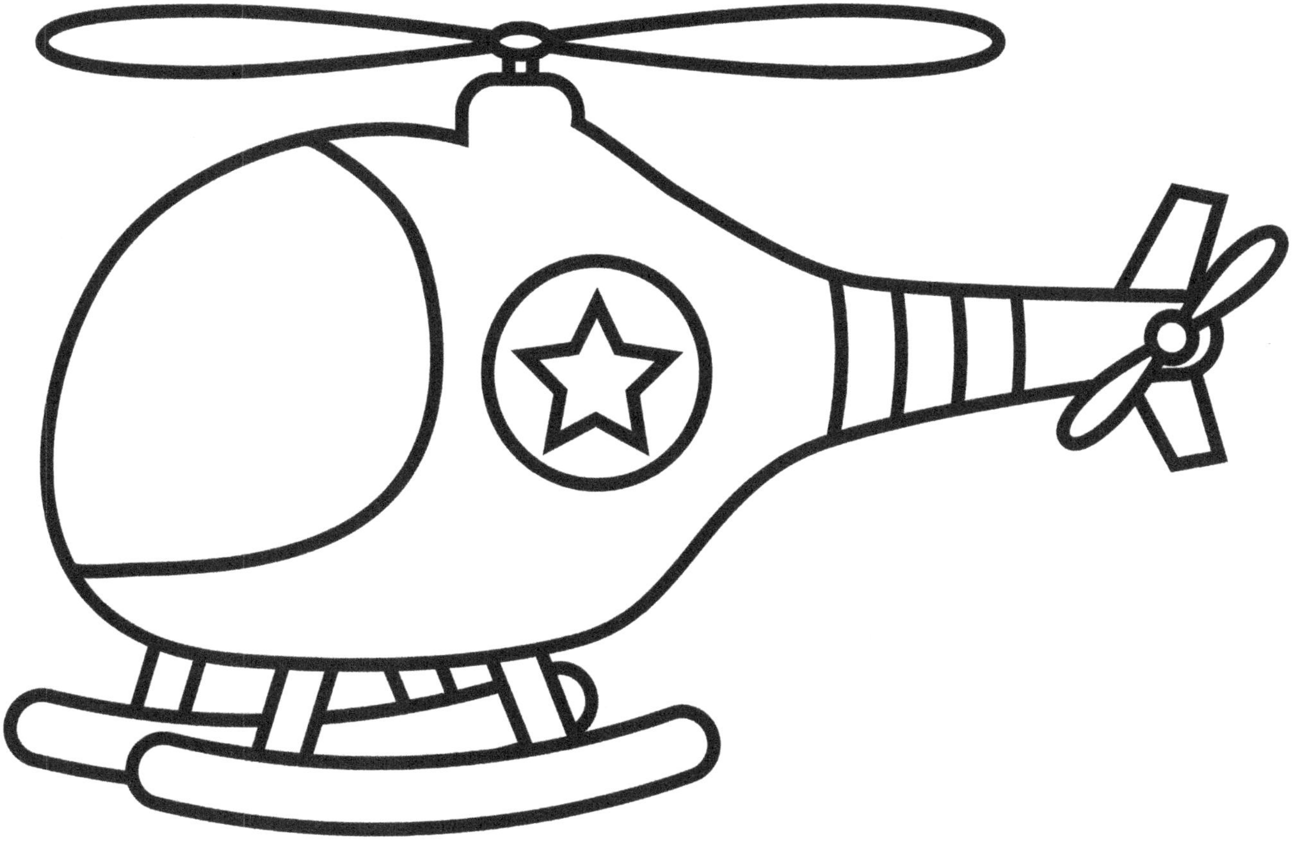

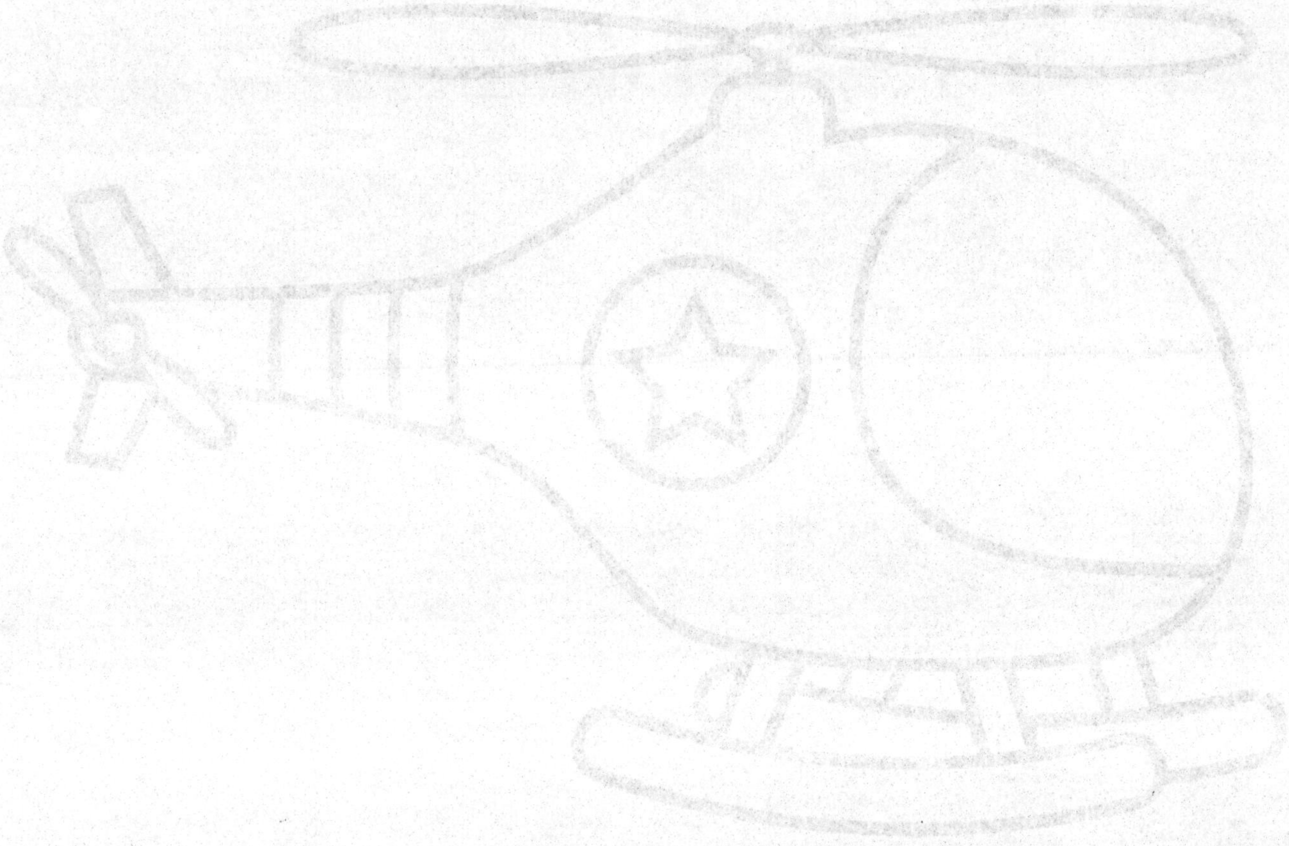

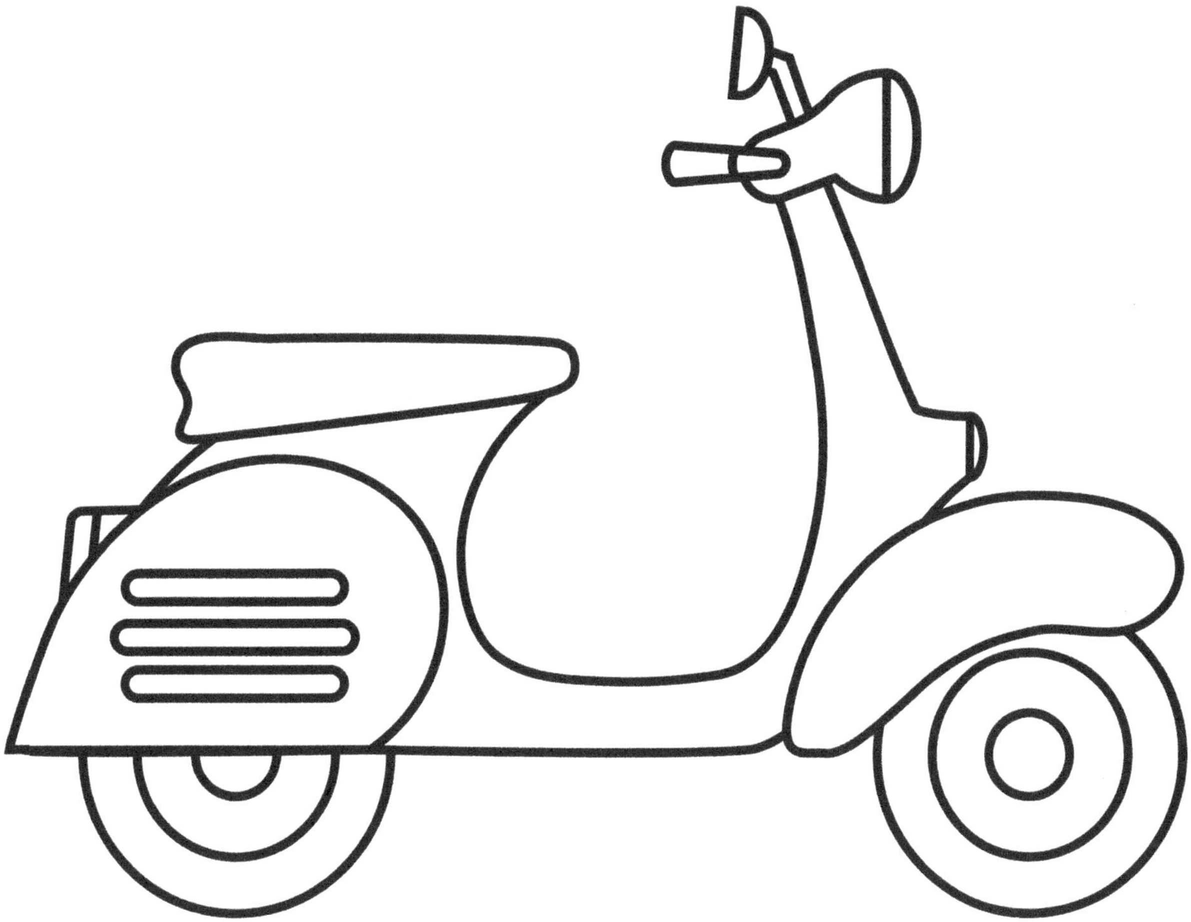

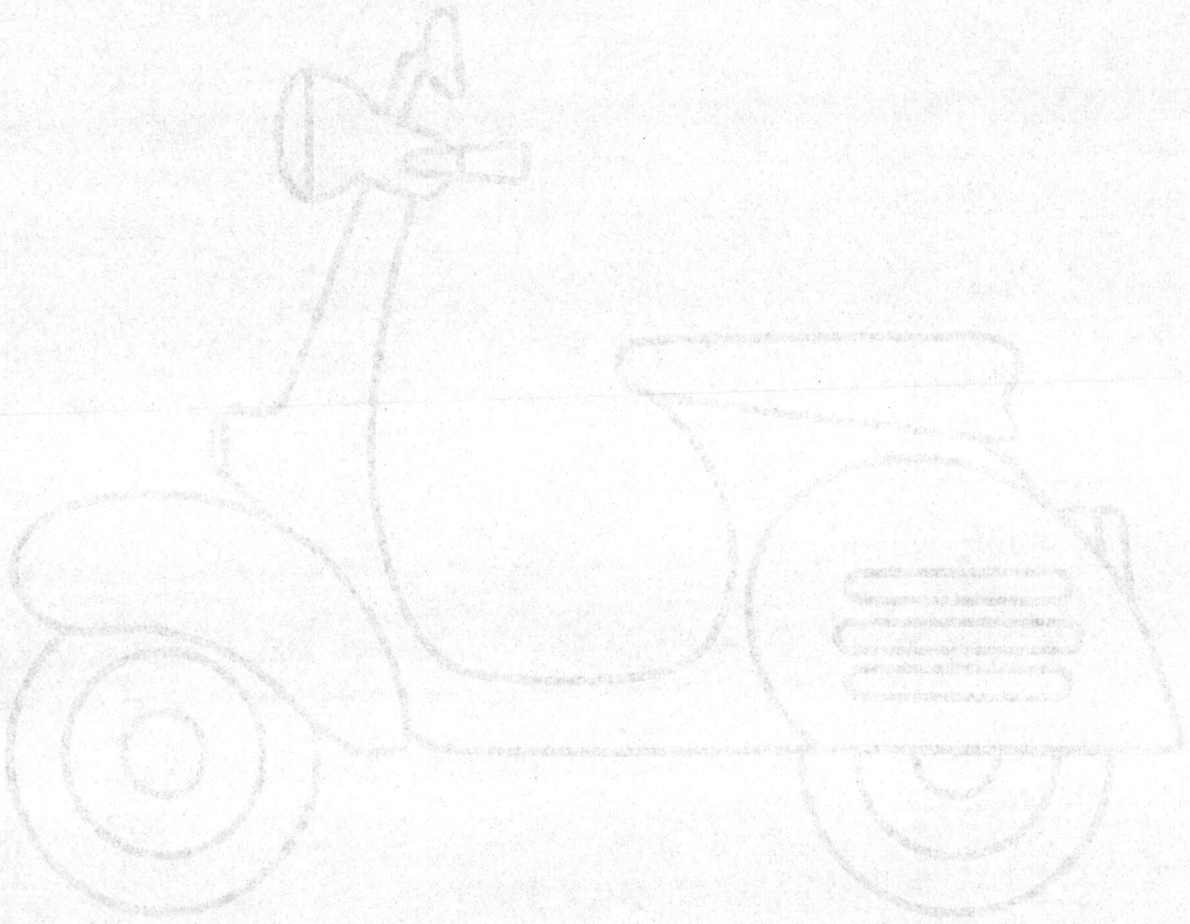

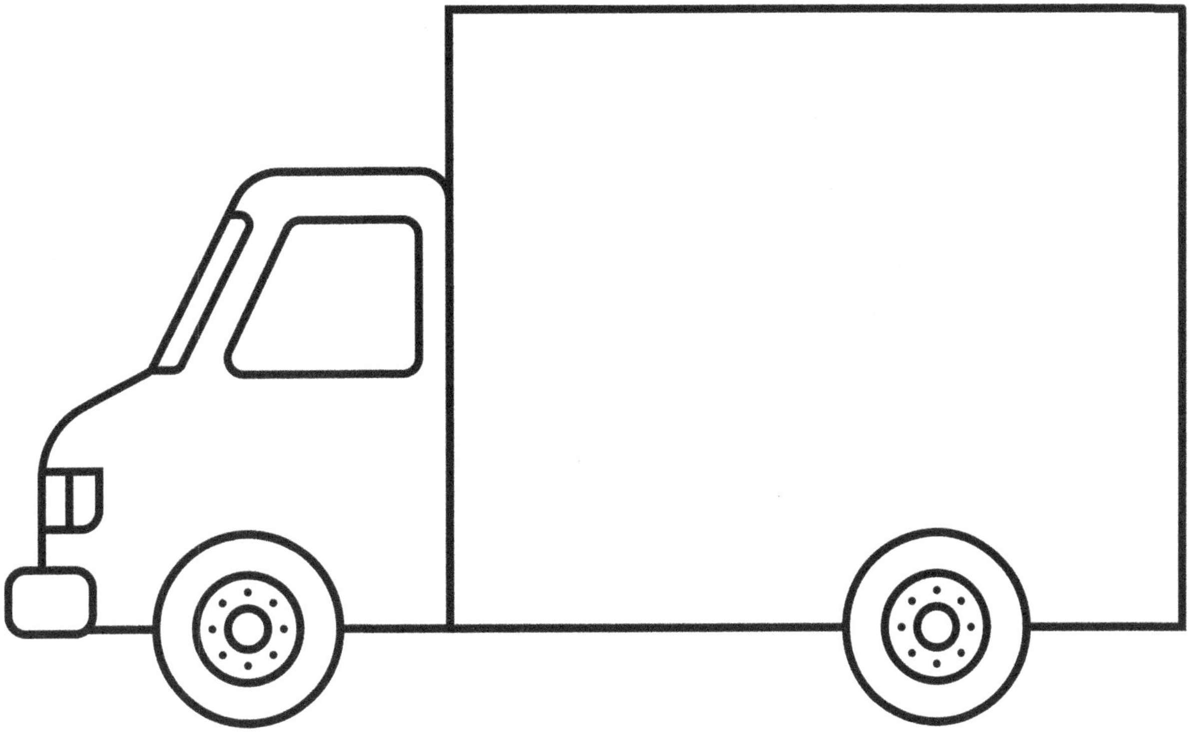

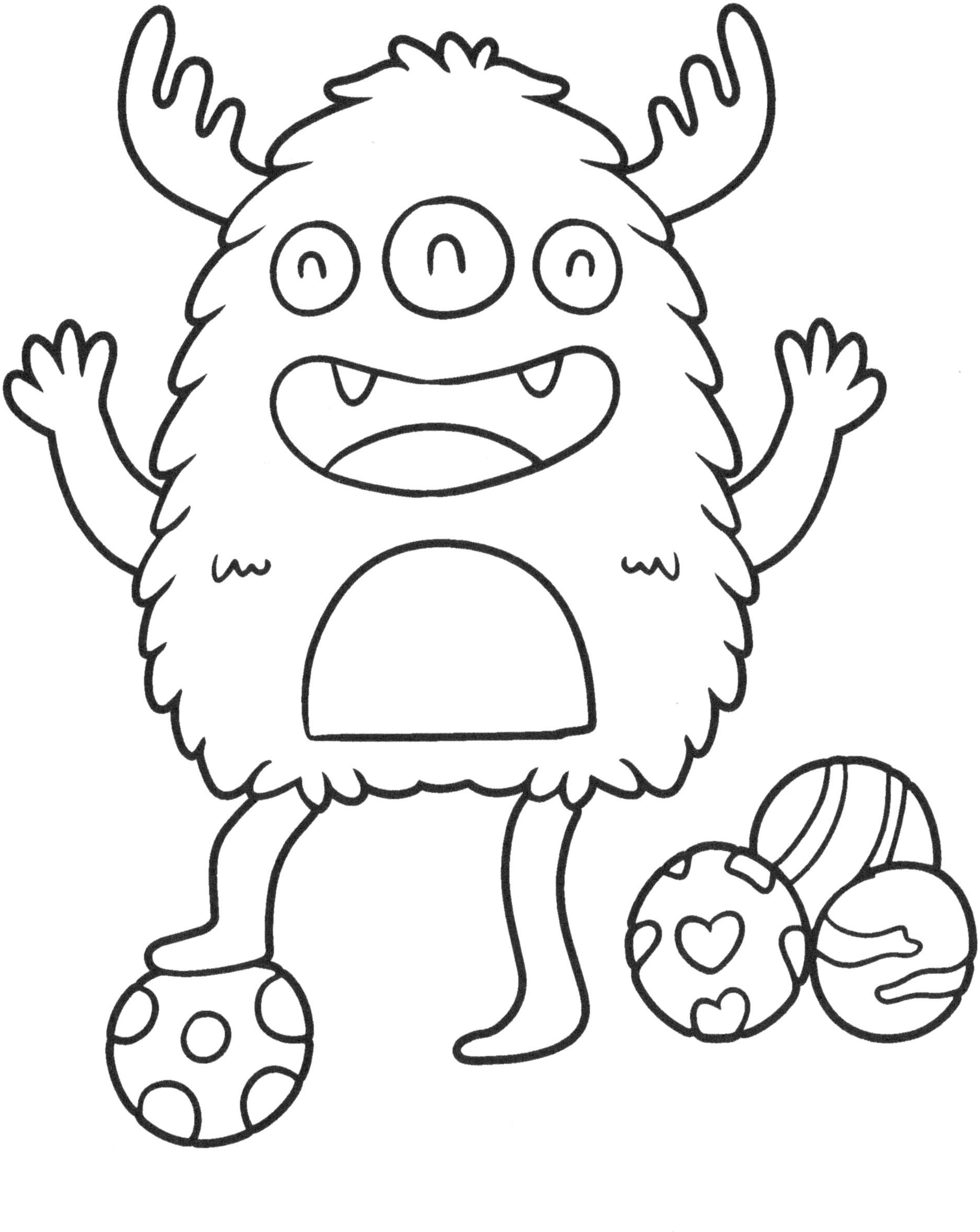

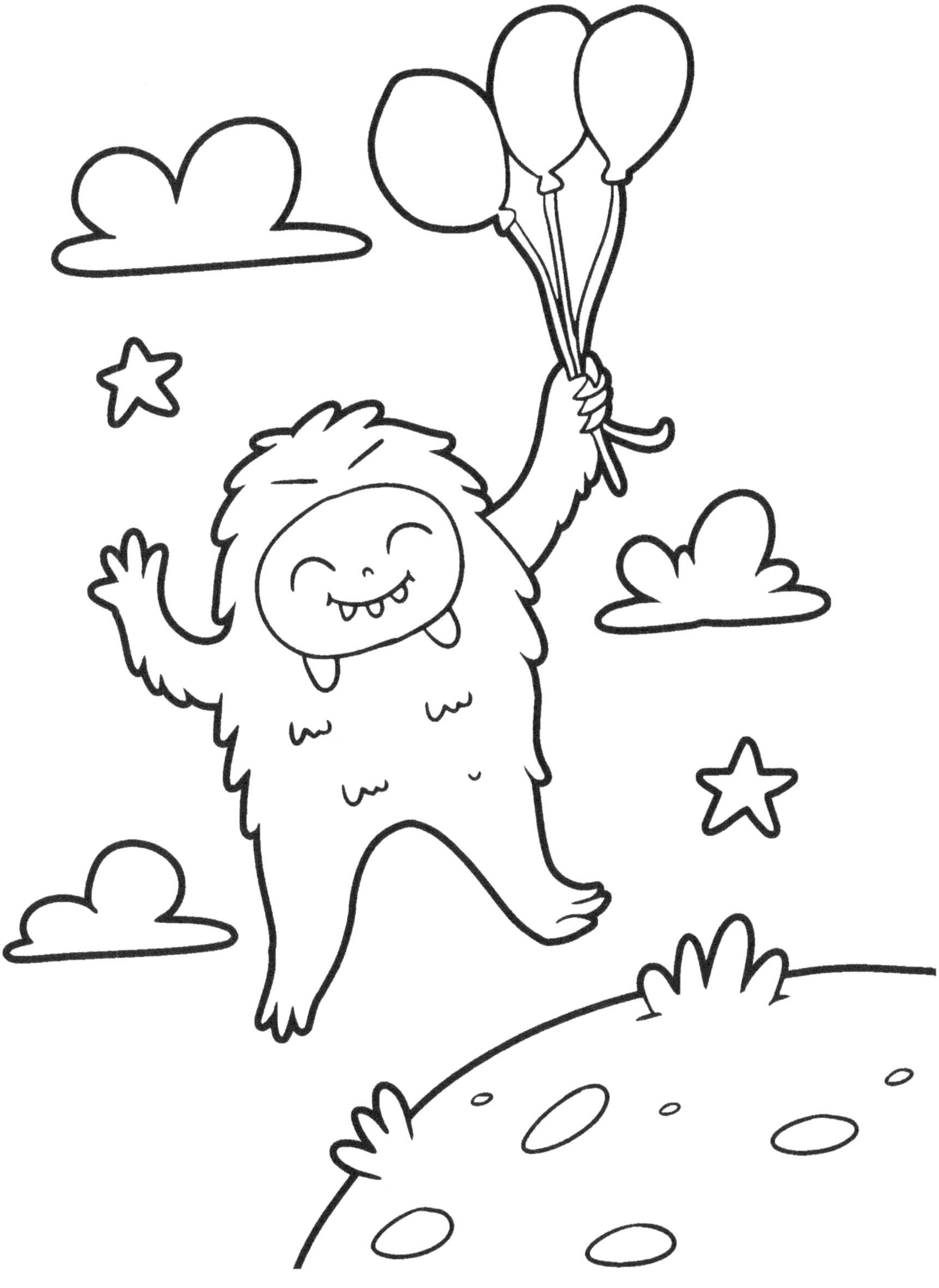

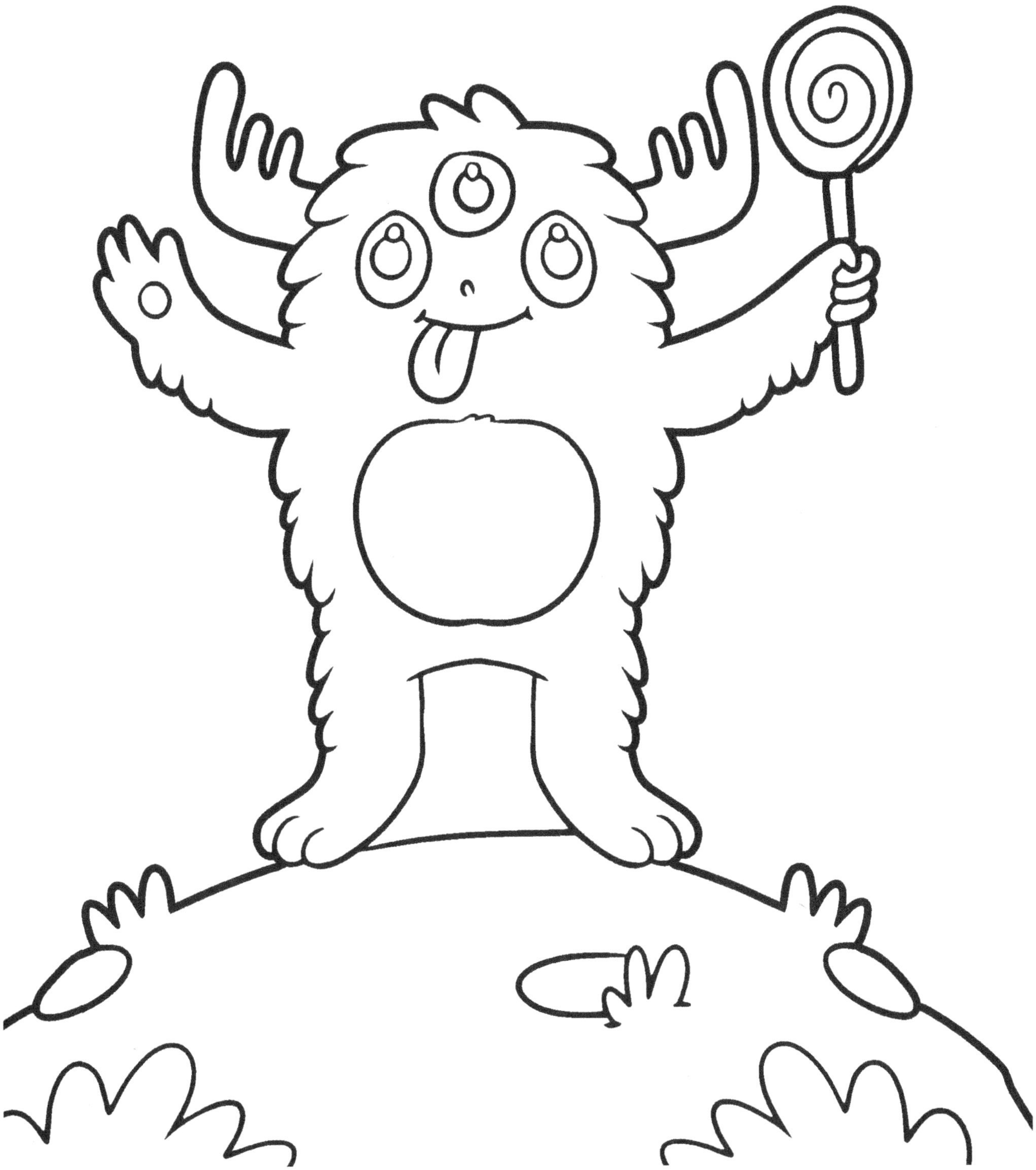

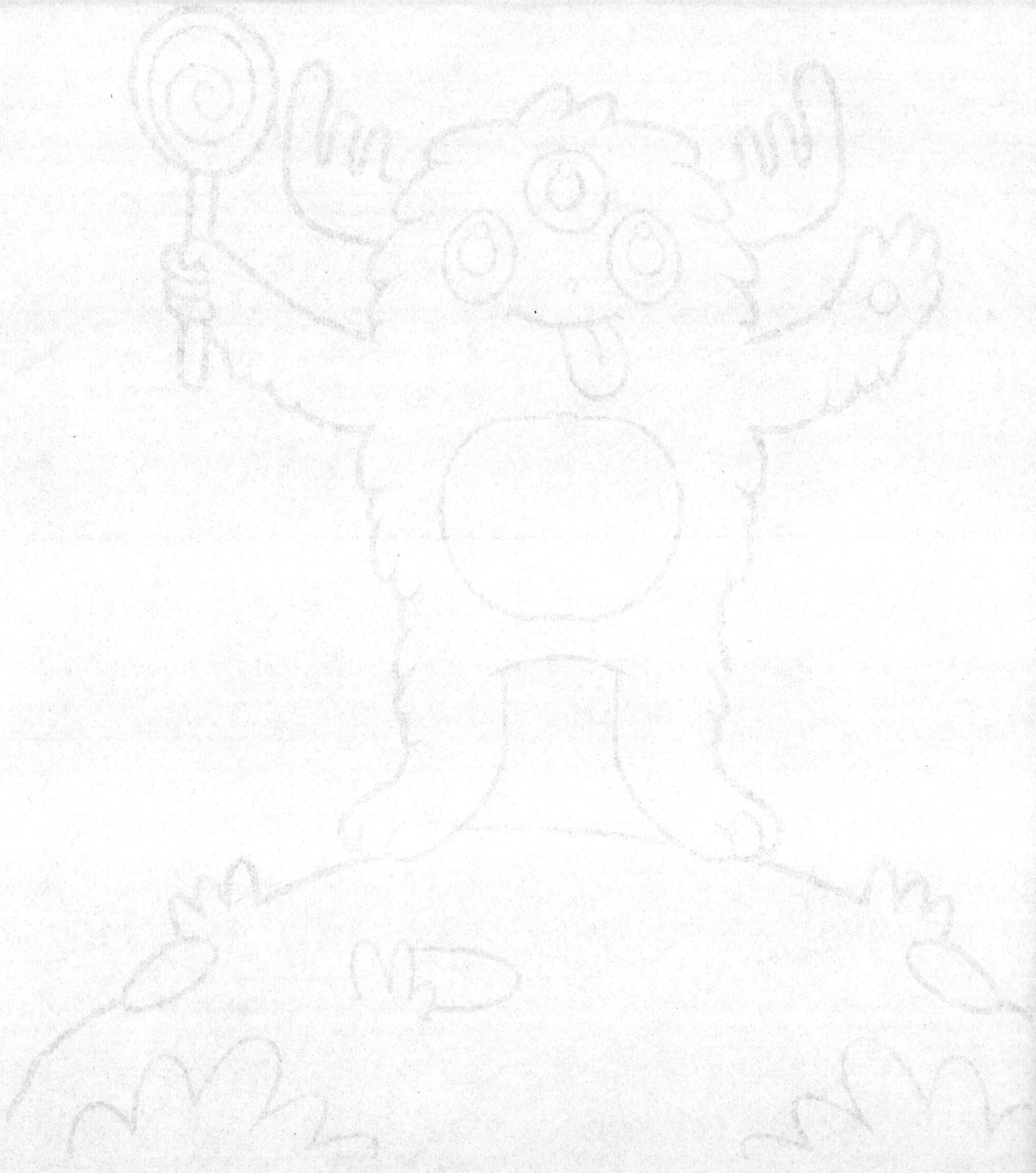

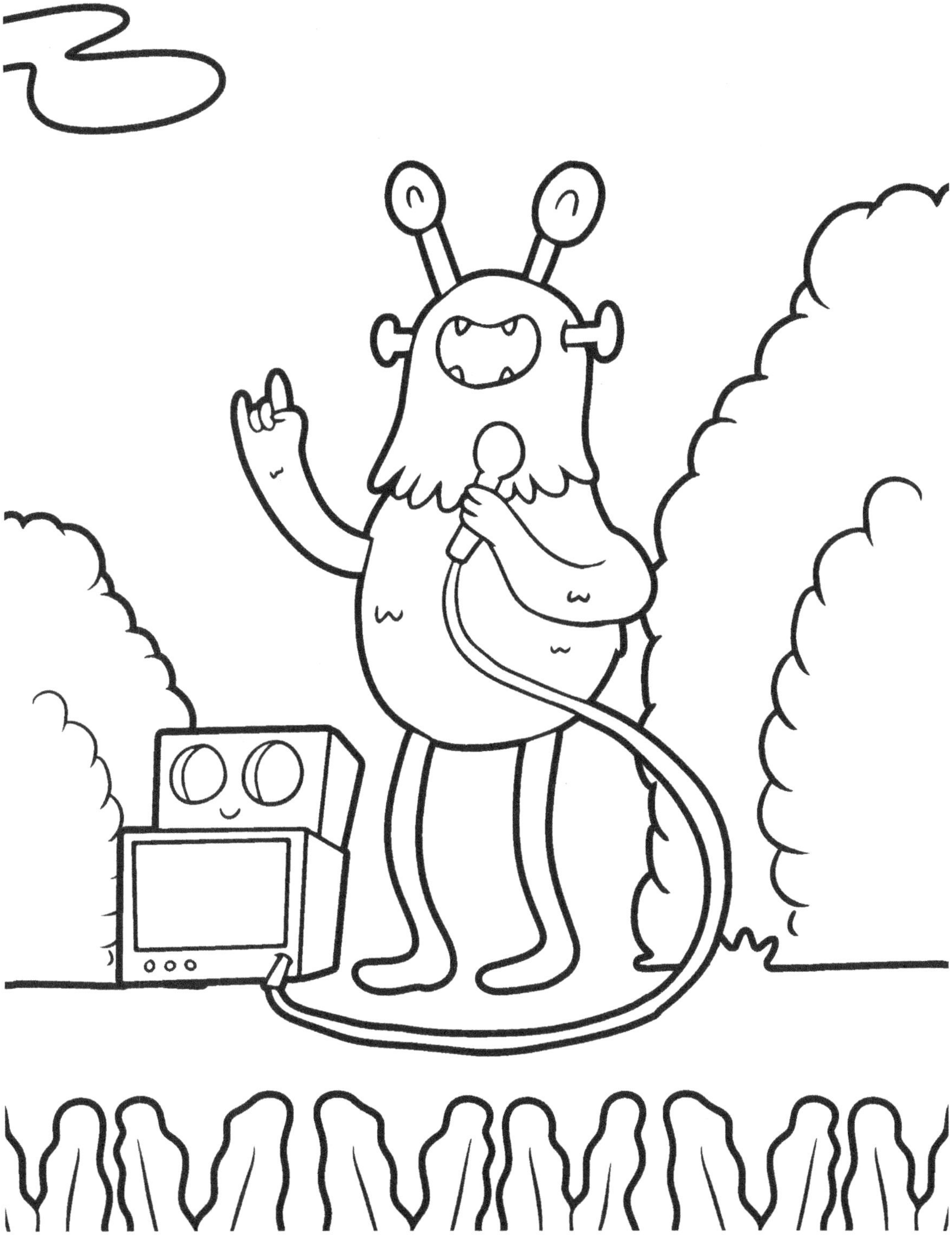

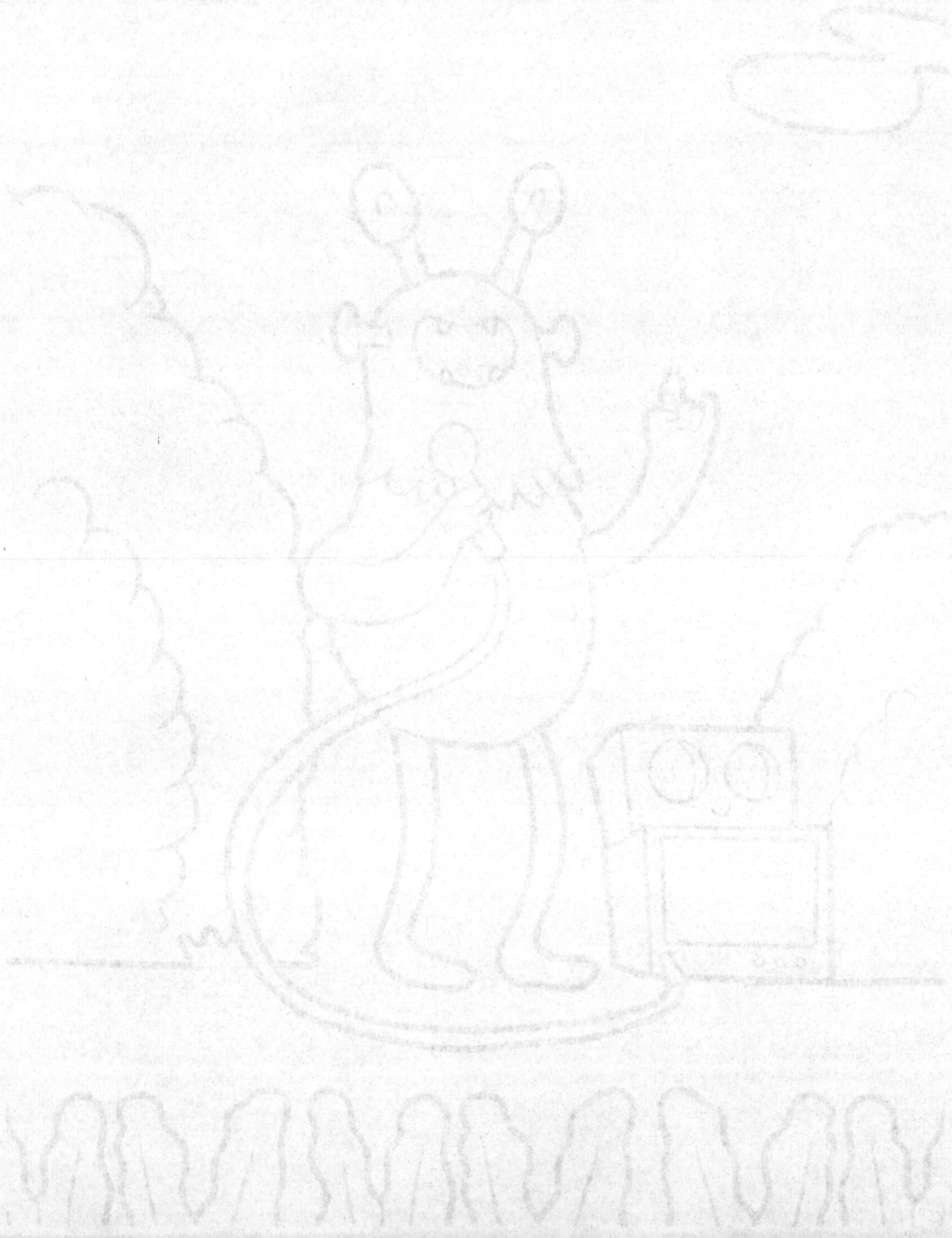

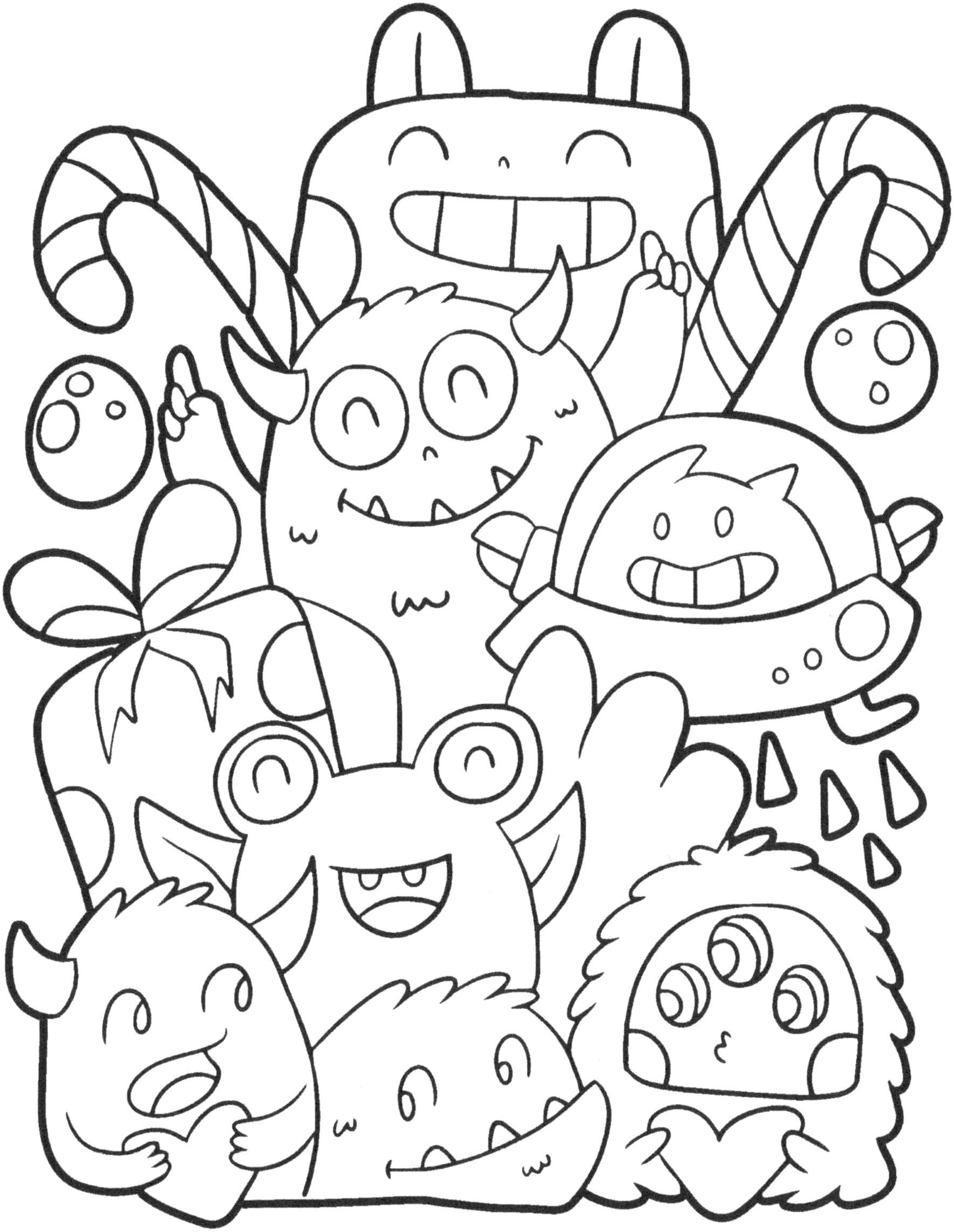

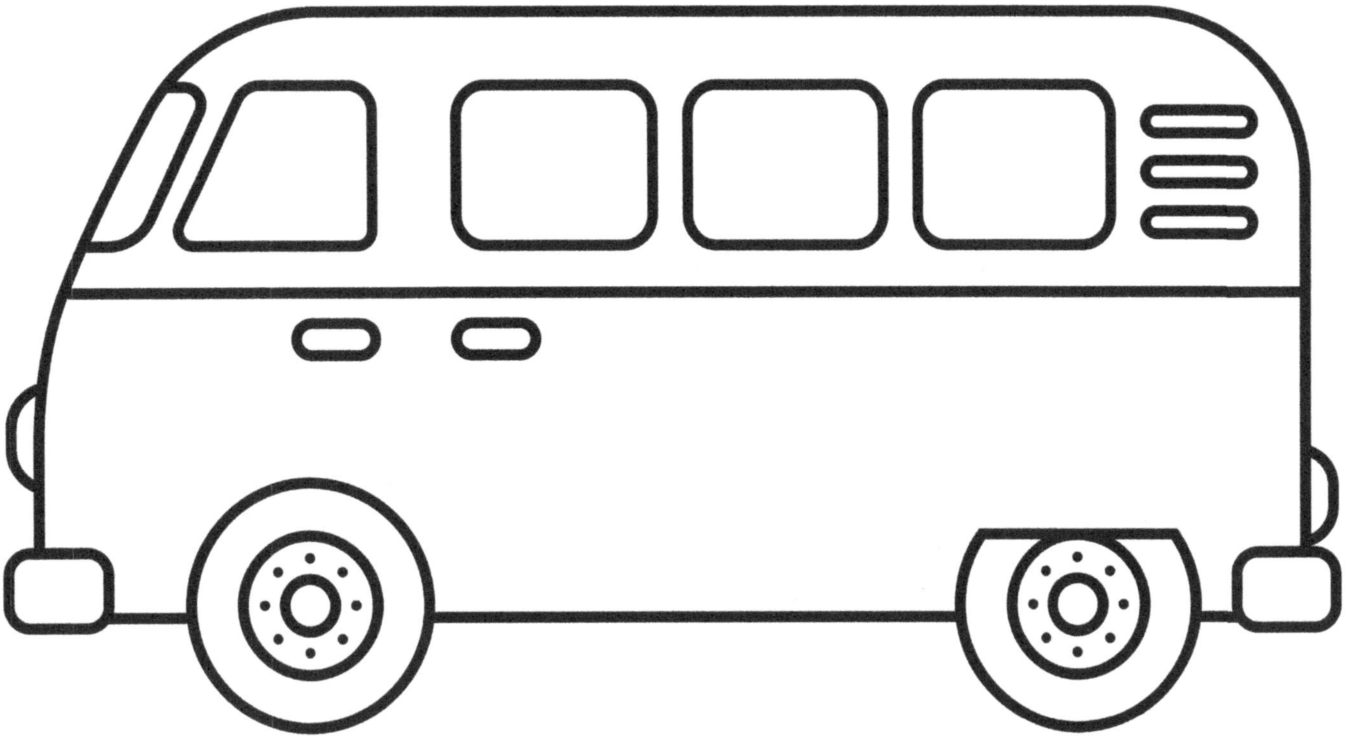

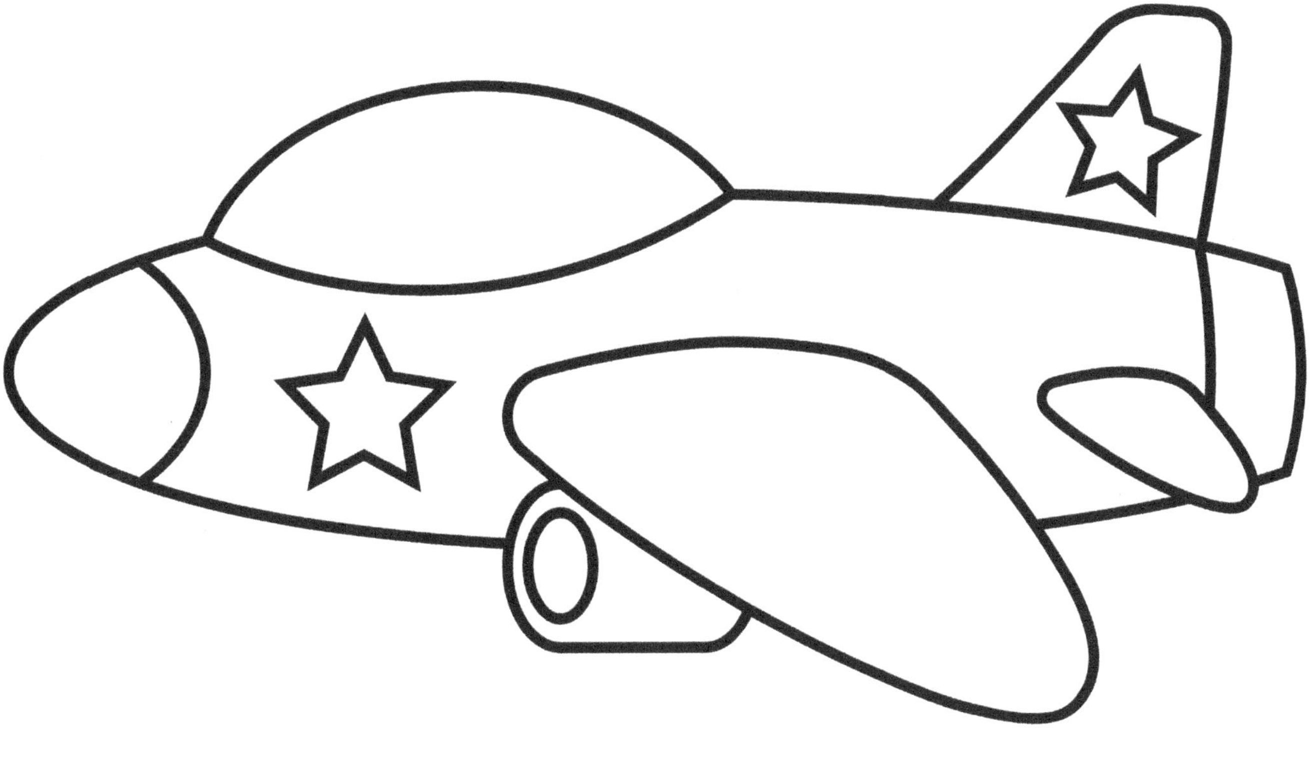

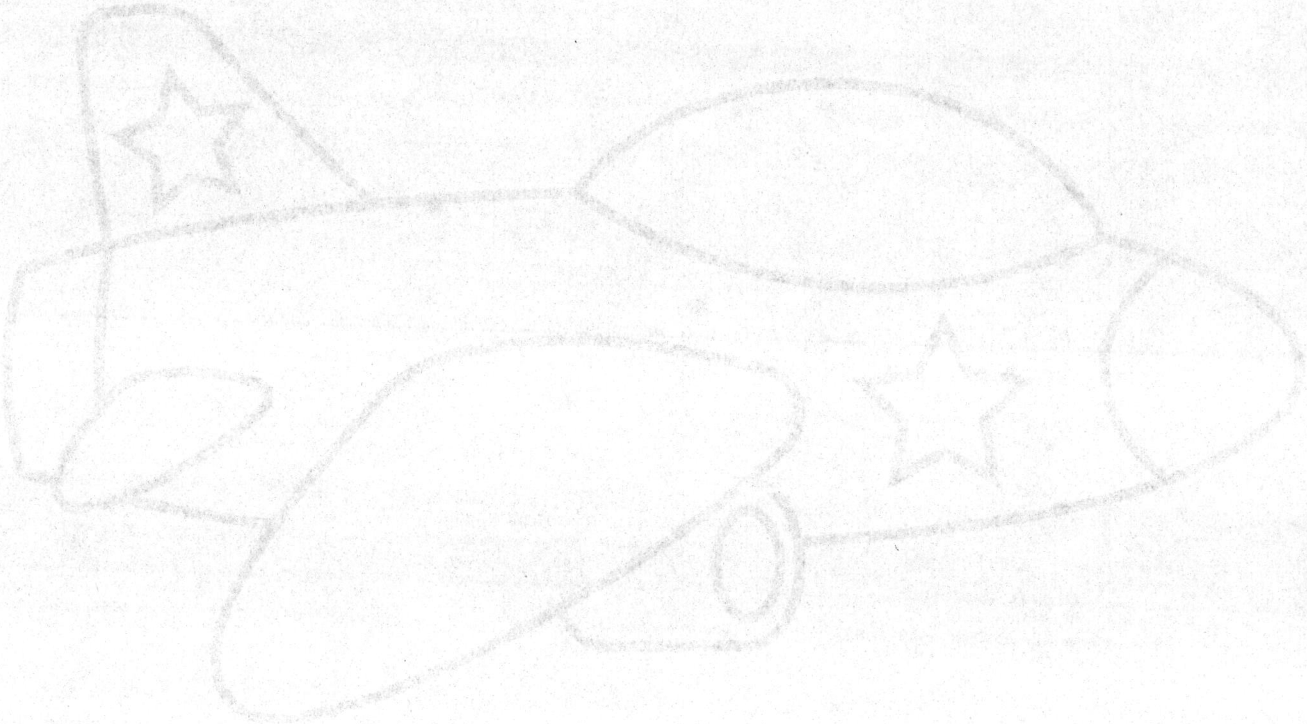

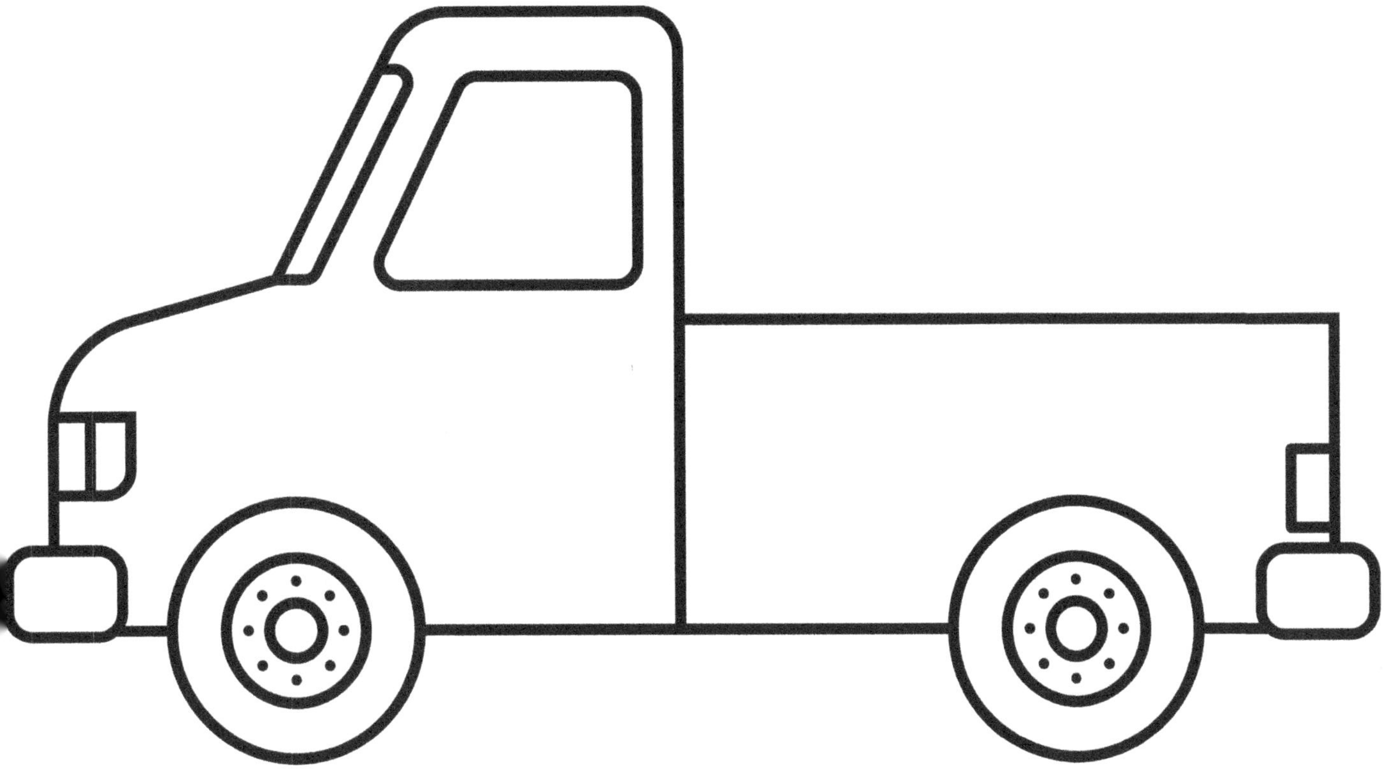

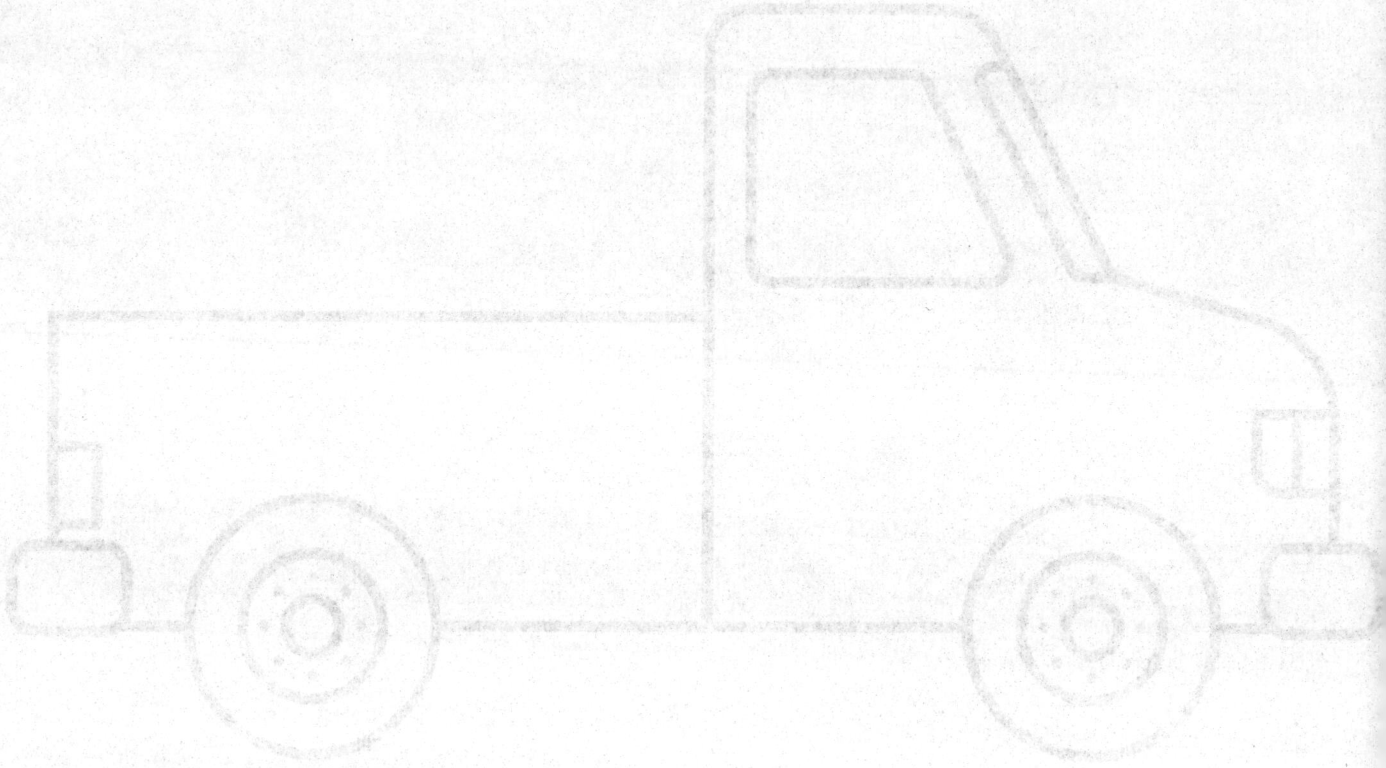

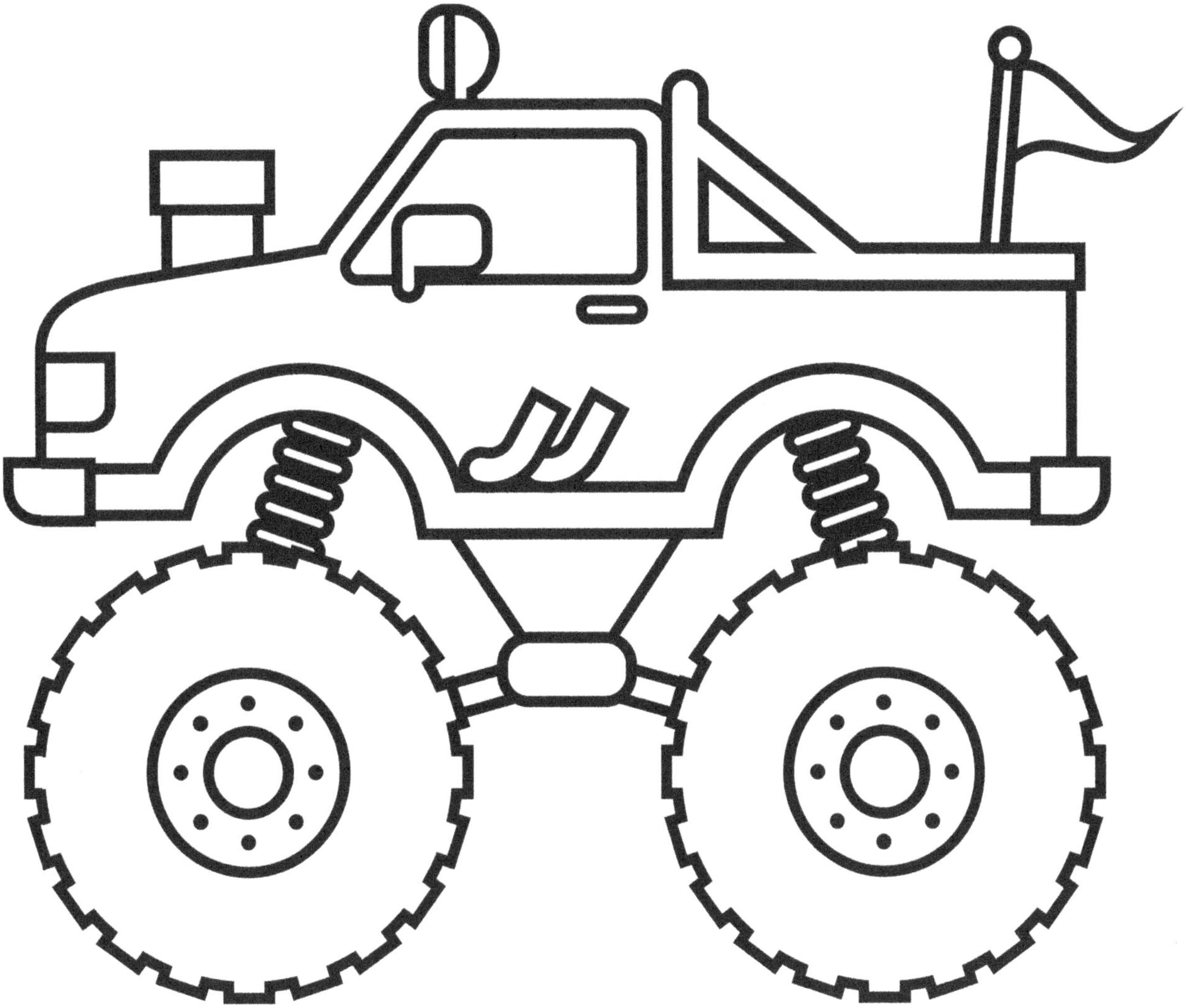

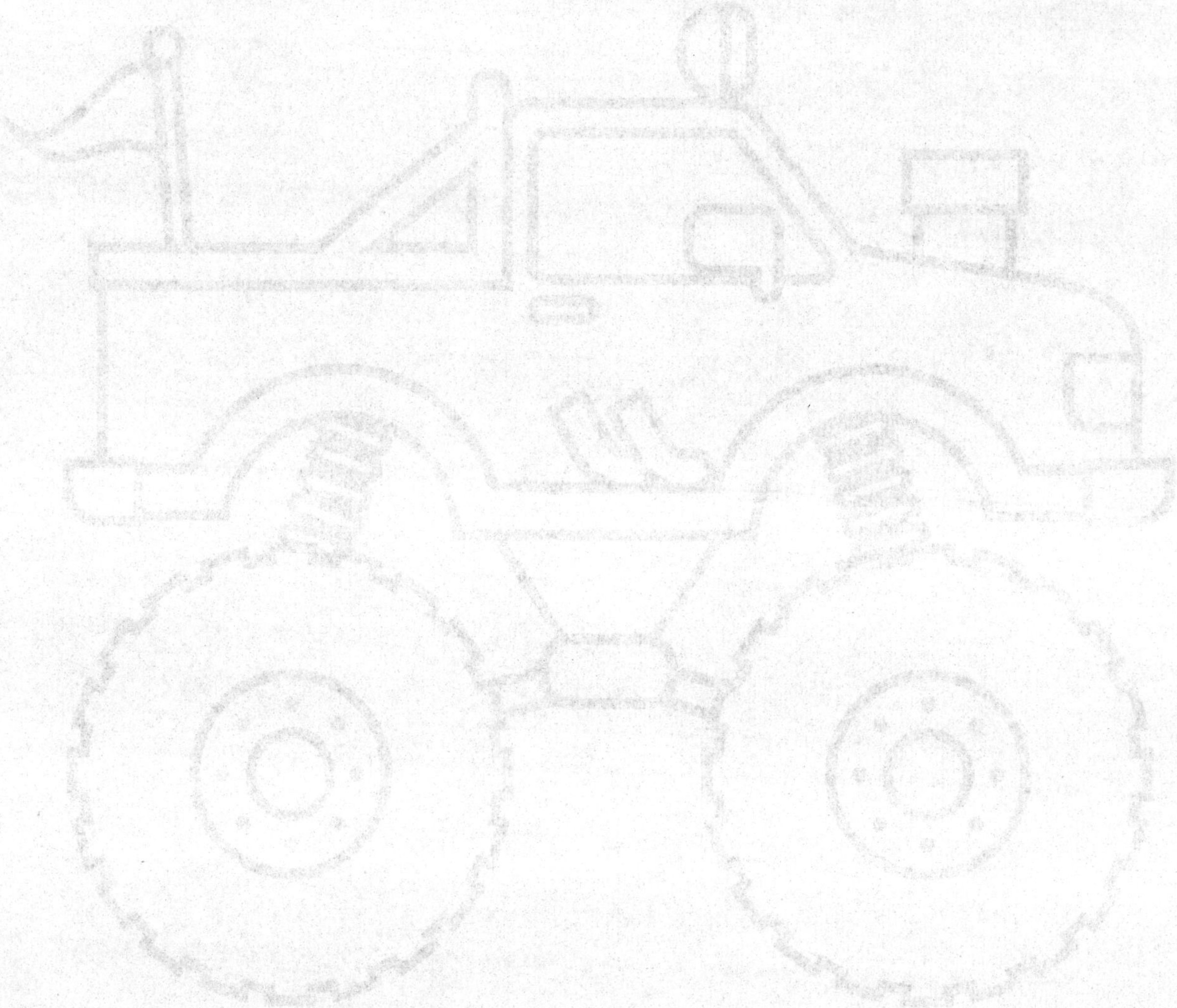

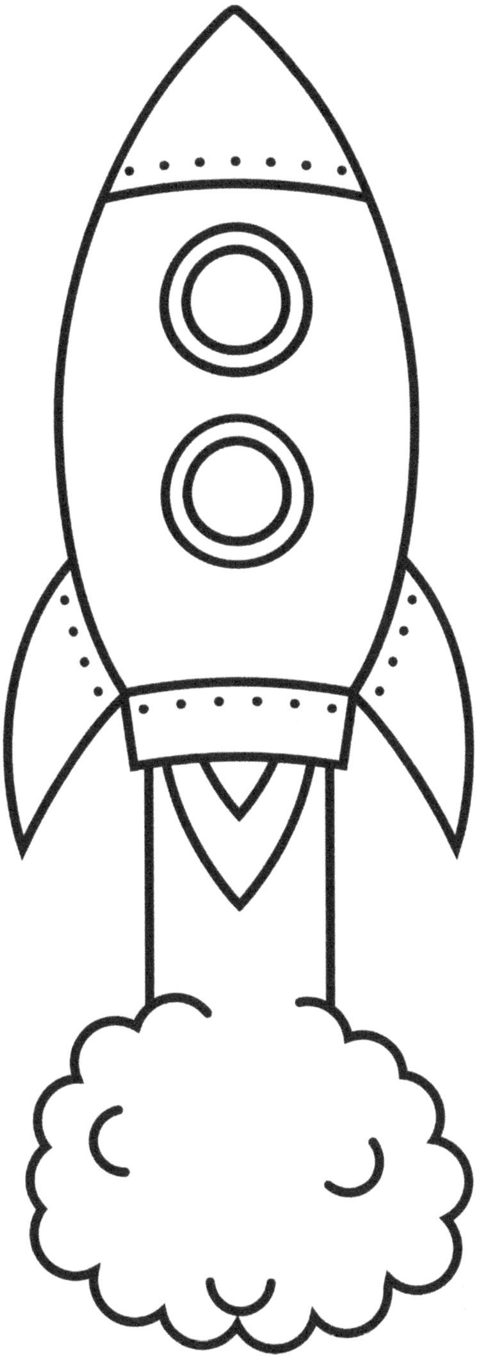

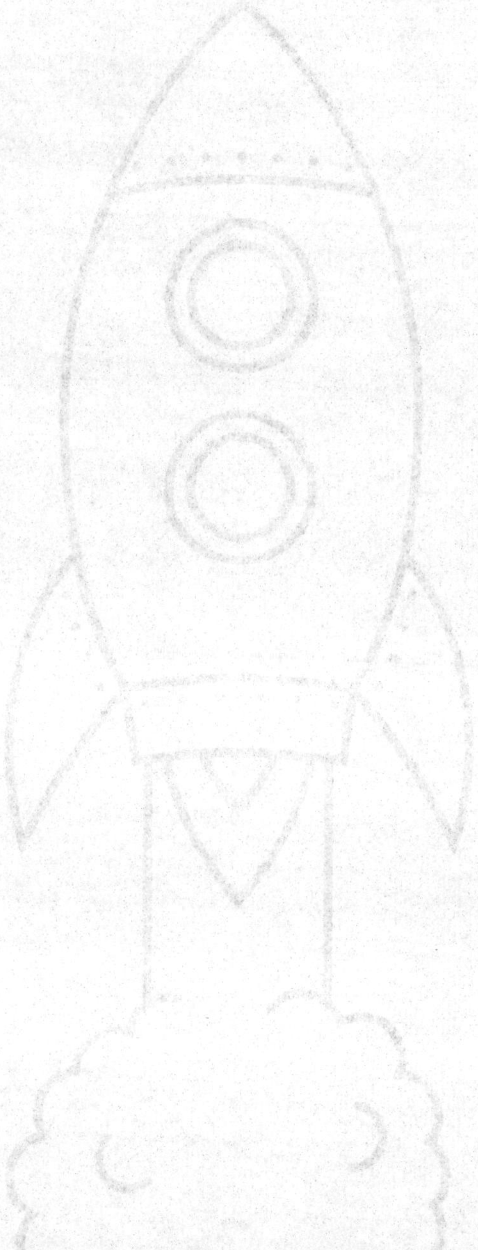

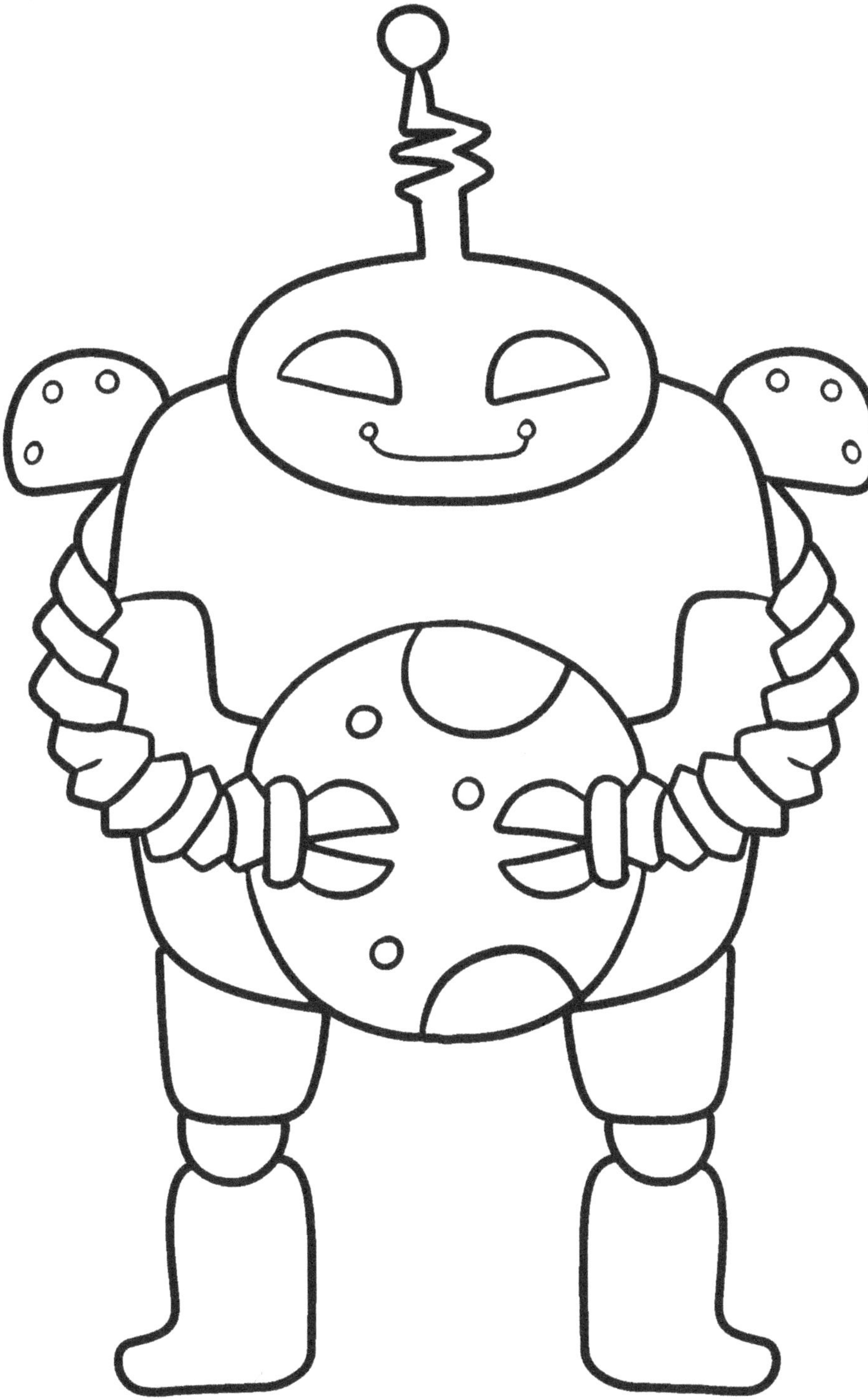

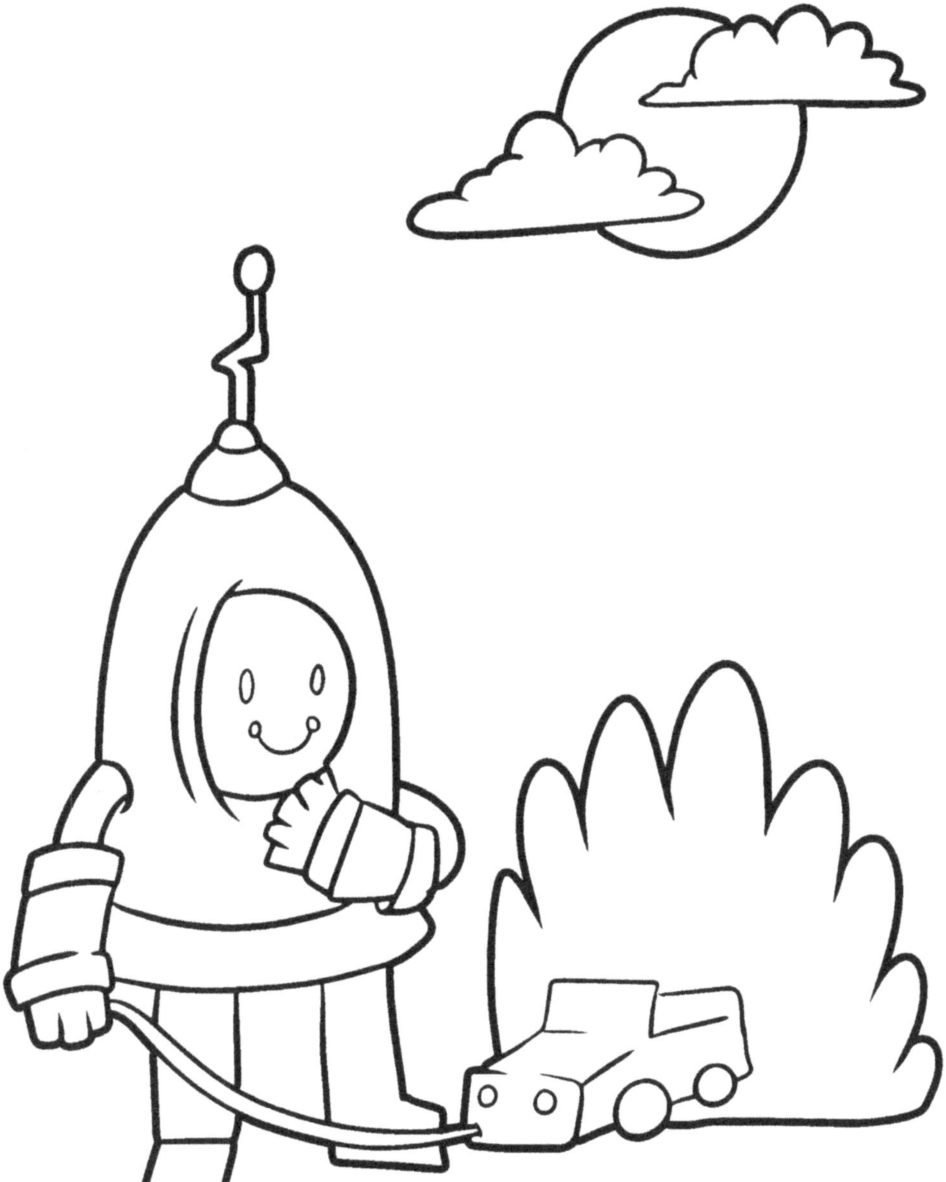

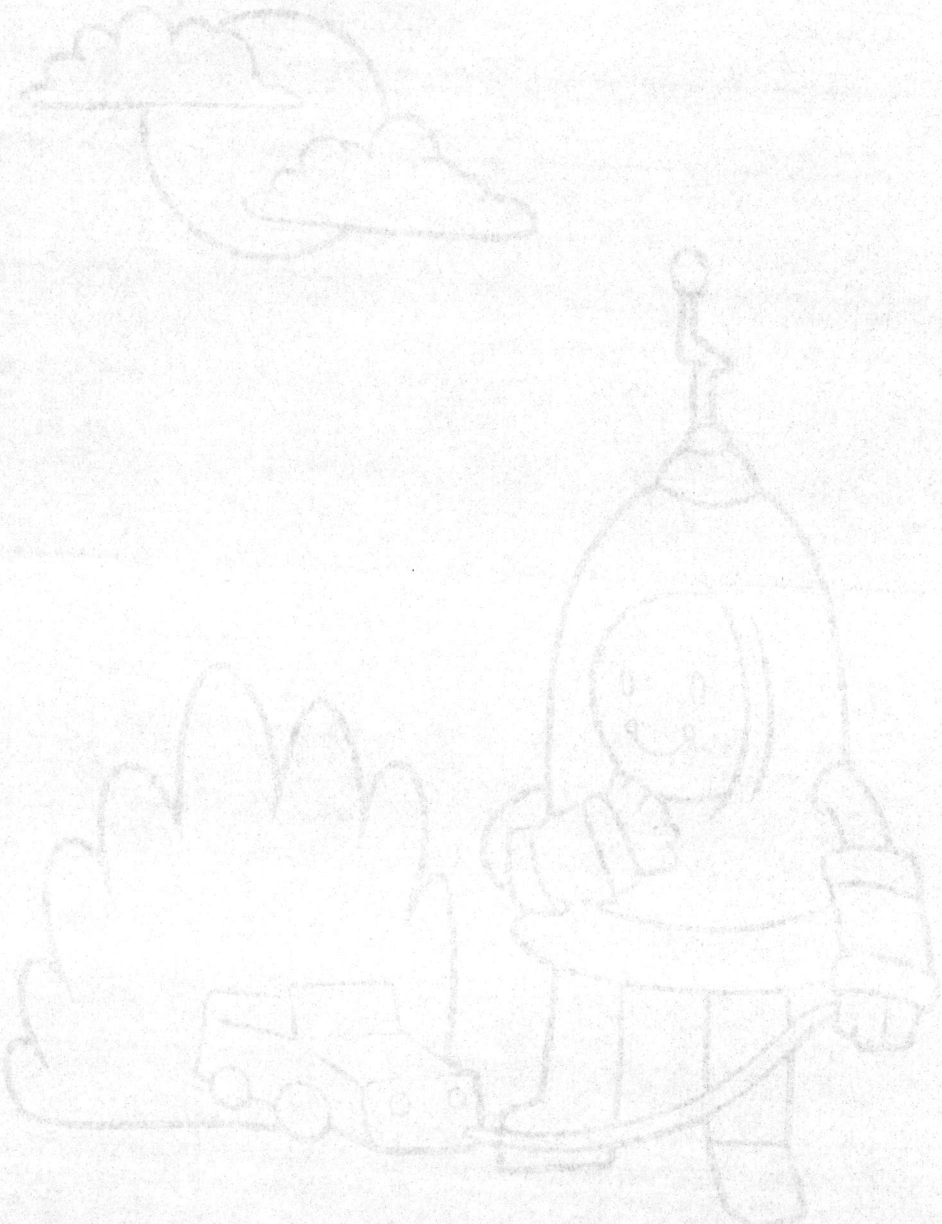

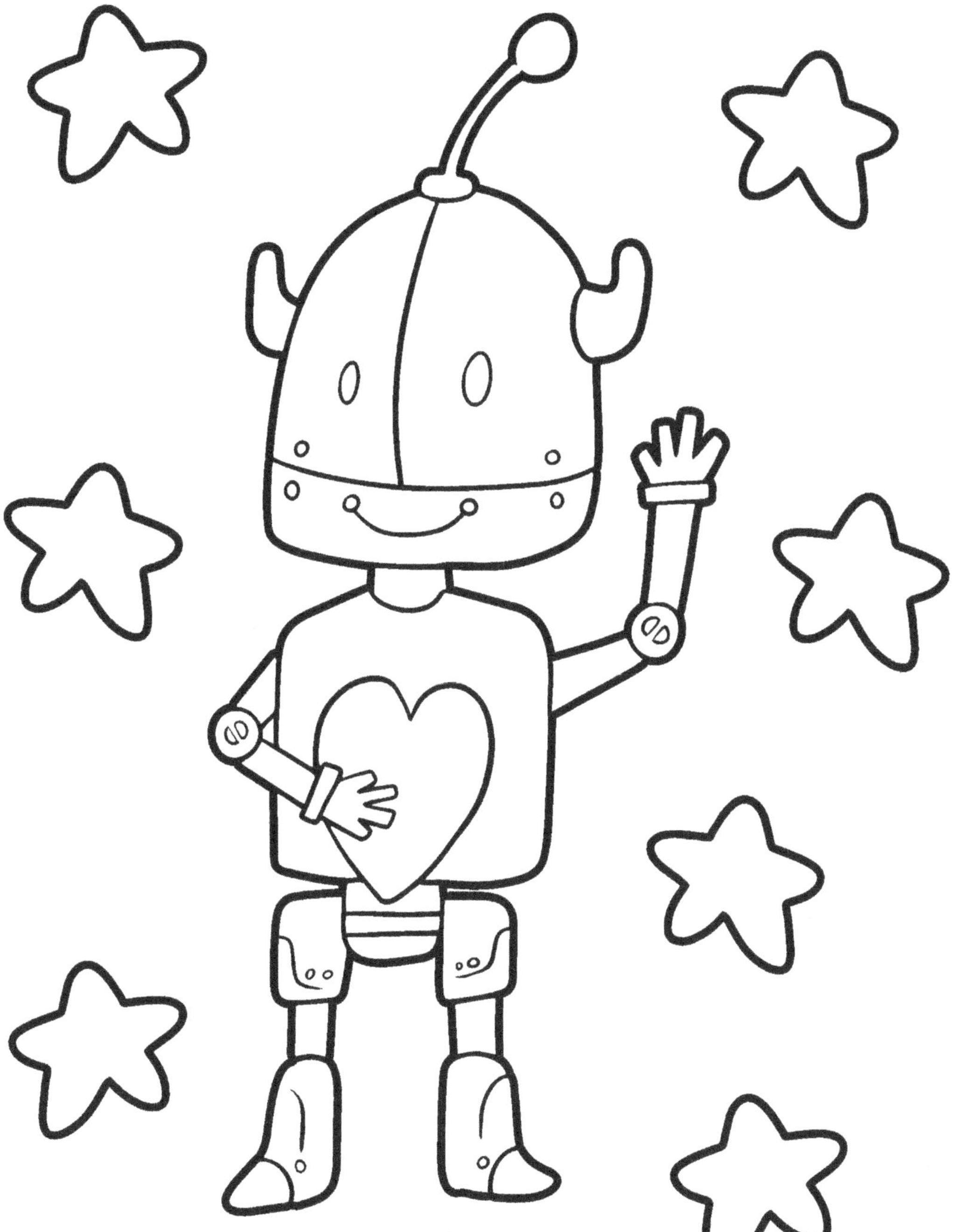

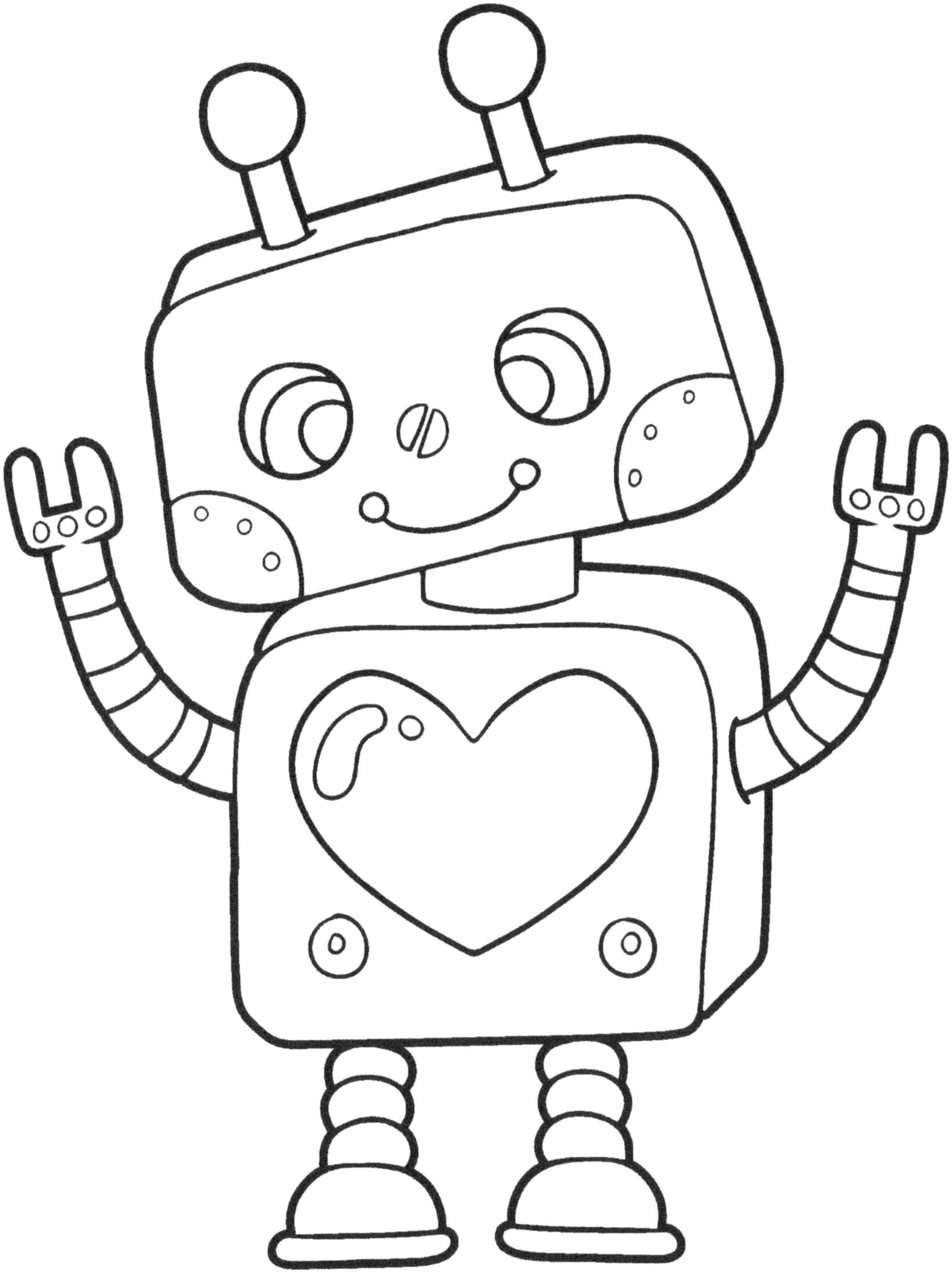

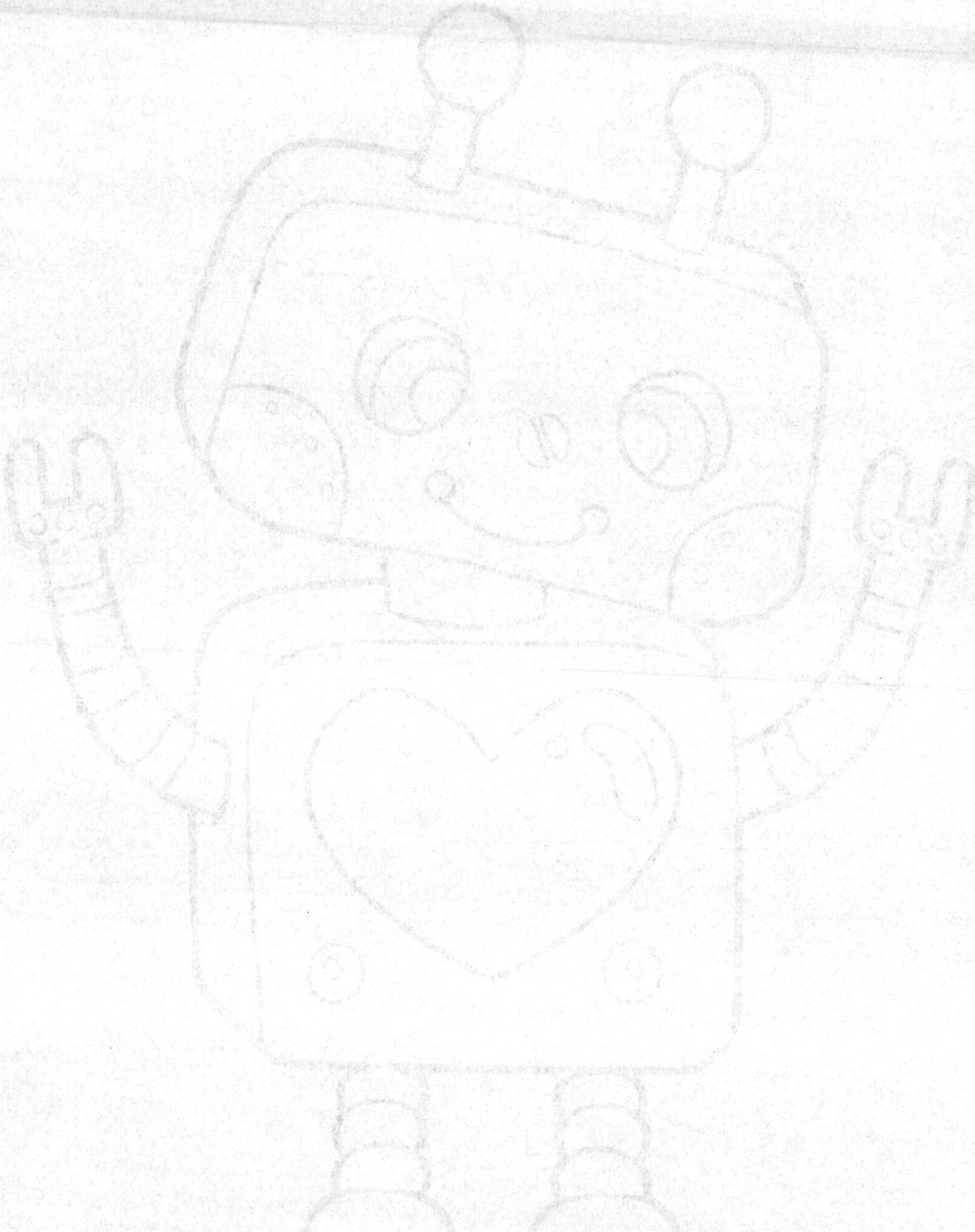

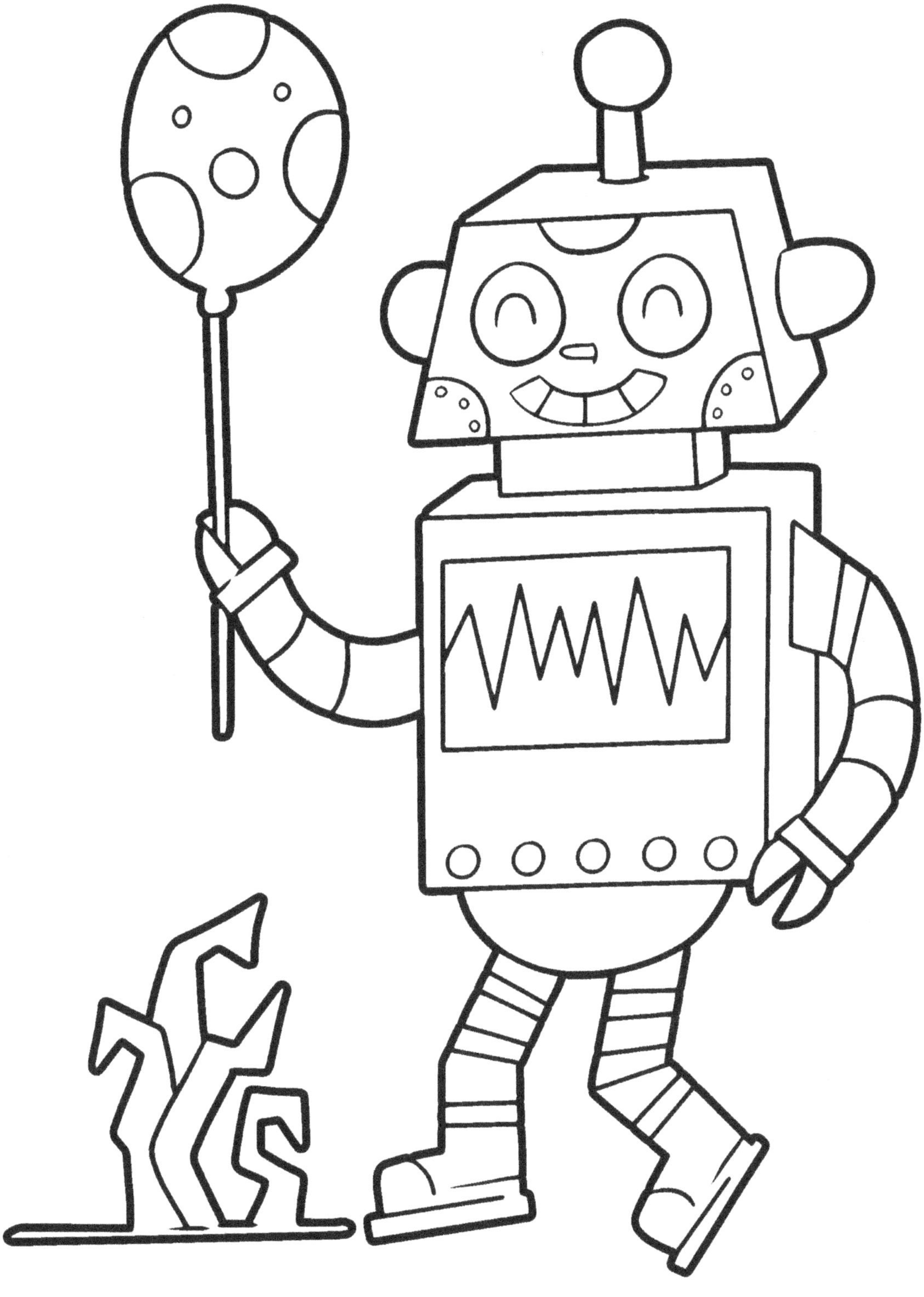

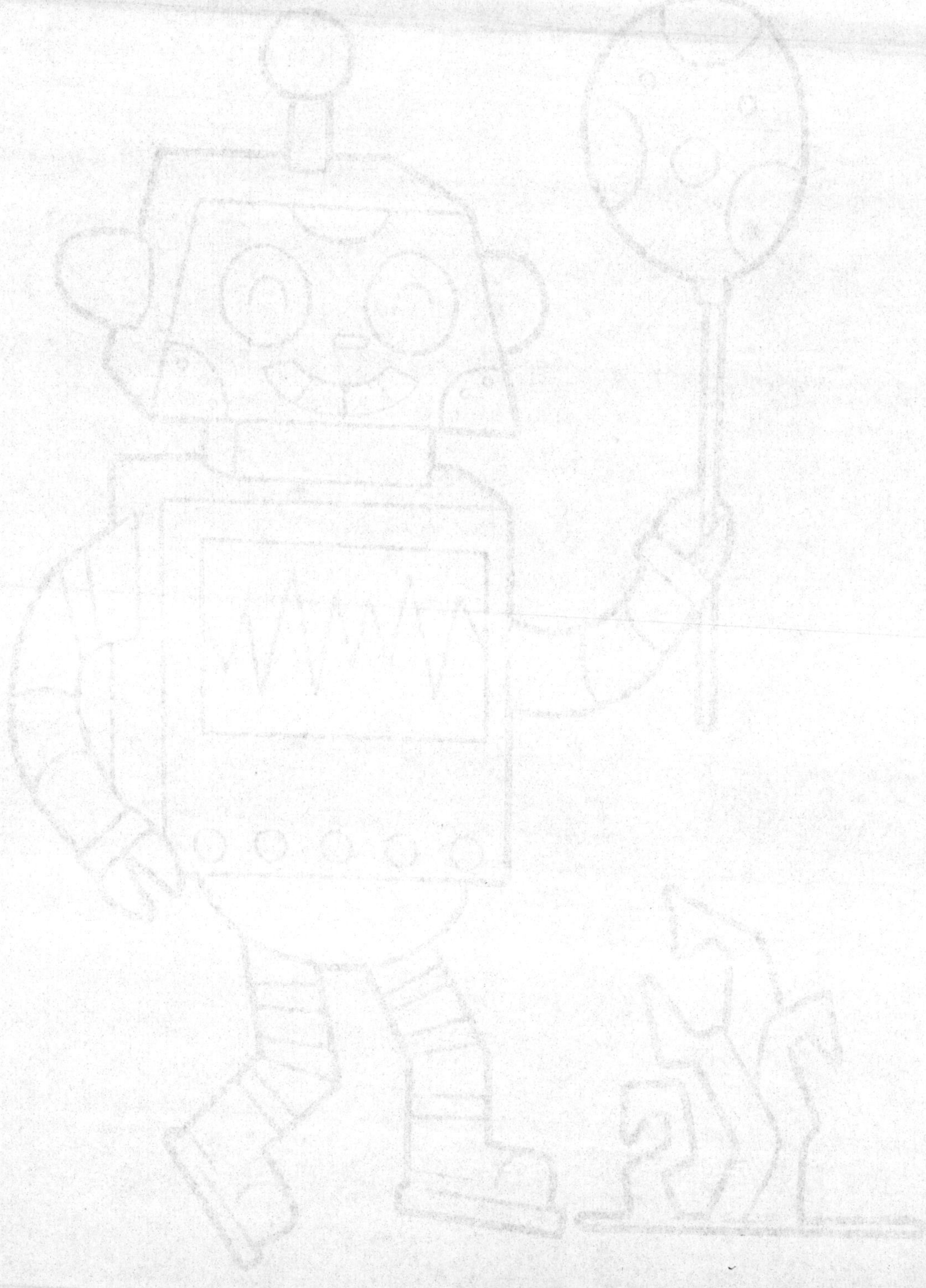

Made in the USA
Las Vegas, NV
24 November 2024

12532221R00031